CONTENTS

PETE WATERMAN

THE FAME FACTOR

Ian Allan

Edited and researched by Sally Atkins

Special thanks to Helen Dann

My personal thanks to: Martin Faulks, Nick Grant, Mark Beynon, Hilary Shaw, Terry Blamey, Carol Hayes, Paul Domaine, Chloe Butcher and Tom Parker.

Pete Waterman's website (thanks to Lee Ashton):
www.pwl-empire.com

The Fame Factor
Pete Waterman

First published 2009
ISBN 978 0 7110 3411 2

© Ian Allan Publishing Ltd 2010

Published by Ian Allan Publishing

an imprint of Ian Allan Publishing Ltd, Hersham, Surrey KT12 4RG.
Printed in England by CPI Mackays, Chatham ME5 8TD

Visit the Ian Allan Publishing website at www.ianallanpublishing.com

INTRODUCTION

So what is this Fame Factor?

If I had a pound for every time someone has asked me "Pete, how do you know when someone's got what it takes?" I would be considerably richer than I am today. By 'what it takes' they mean of course the talent to become a famous star; and until someone asked me to write this book I can honestly say that I hadn't consciously analysed what that is, even when I was arguing with Simon Cowell on the panel of Pop Idol!

99 times out of a 100 I can tell pretty quickly whether or not a hopeful young artist has any chance of achieving success. However, when I first sat down to write I realised that although part of my ability to spot talent is pure instinct, that ability is also based on years of experience. When I look at a new artist what I actually do is subconsciously apply a set of requirements and see how they measure up. Their resulting score is their Fame Factor.

Take a look at my Fame Factor Grid and the ten pop icons I have chosen to score on it. The names of the stars are down the side of the grid and the Fame Factors across the top.

It works like this: if you think that Beyoncé has a 'Distinctive Voice' put a star in the box where those two lines meet. I've started you off by scoring Kylie a perfect 10. Fill in the whole of the grid like this, giving each icon a star for each of the Fame Factors you think the icon has, and then add up their score on the right hand side of the grid. Who do you think should get full marks and who 'could do better'?

You'll also see that I have filled in a bold star for each of my icons. These indicate that I have chosen that artist as a perfect example of that Fame Factor.

In the following chapters I explain exactly what I mean by each of these Fame Factors. I also discover which of my icons have gaps in their CV's; believe me they don't all score a perfect 10 when all is revealed on the Fame Factor grid at the end of the book!

THE FAME FACTOR GRID

★ The 10 Fame Factor elements are listed at the top of the grid.

★ Put a star in the box for each of the elements you think the pop icon has.

★ Add up the Fame Factor scores in the right hand column.

	1. The Songs	2. A Distinctive Voice	3. The Look	4. Determin- ation	5. Stamina
Michael Jackson	★				
Madonna		★			
Lady Gaga			★		
Simon Cowell				★	
Kylie Minogue	☆	☆	☆	☆	★
Spice Girls					
Robbie Williams					
Girls Aloud					
Beyonce Knowles					
Leona Lewis					
YOU					

★ I've started you off by giving Kylie a perfect 10.

★ Now work out your own Fame Factor score in the row left blank for you to fill in.

★ The bold stars show the artists I have chosen to represent each Fame Factor.

6. PR'ability	7. Self Belief	8. Supporting Cast	9. Killer Moves	10. Public Appeal	Fame Factor Score
☆	☆	☆	☆	☆	10
★					
	★				
		★			
			★		
				★	

However, the real purpose of this book is to help you to discover whether *you've* got what it takes. That's why there's a row for you to fill in and rate your own Fame Factor, to see how you measure up against some real stars and whether you are missing any crucial elements.

I'll throw in some quizzes along the way to test your music knowledge and help you to figure out which of the Fame Factors you have already, and how can you improve on any you are lacking.

You might even decide that the whole pursuit of fame is, in reality, just too much hard work! Even if you do, this book will provide you with hours of fun and entertaining debate as you score your friends, your fellow band members and your own favourite stars on the Fame Factor grid!

THE 10 FAME FACTOR ELEMENTS...

So here's a summary of the 10 crucial Fame Factor elements featured on the grid that you will need if you are going to beat the thousands of other young hopefuls to fame and fortune.

1. The Songs

Surprised? I bet you thought that the first Fame Factor ingredient was going to be talent! Well we'll get to that in a minute, but let's be honest, you can have the greatest voice in the world but no-one, except perhaps your mum and dad and your grandma, is going to buy a truly dreadful song. And even your grandma might think twice about spending her pension on your version of 'Agadoo'.

And yes, it's songs, plural. What's the point in expending all that time and energy on getting to the top of the charts if you turn out to be a one hit wonder!

2. A Distinctive Voice

Notice again that I'm talking about a distinctive voice and not an amazing voice or even a classic voice. Of course you have to be able to sing in tune and in time but the really crucial ingredient is the one that lets people know it's you the minute they hear your record on the radio.

I pull no punches when I analyse some 'great' singers and once you've read this chapter you'll be re-thinking the way you listen to everyone! More importantly it will make you think about your own voice. Whether you have a god-given talent or you've been taking singing lessons since the age of three, this is the moment to really listen to the sound you make when you sing and see what you can do to increase its appeal.

3. The Look

One of the most obvious and yet one of the most controversial Fame Factors. The road to stardom is paved with beautiful people – or is it? It's certainly littered with hundreds of gorgeous hopefuls who fall at the first hurdle.

So what exactly do you need? A classic trademark style or a quirky statement? Beyoncé's legs and Kylie's bottom or Madonna's ability to re-invent her image from one 'striking pose' to the next.

One thing's for sure, most stars would feel traumatised and exposed without their make-up artists, hairdressers, personal trainers and stylists, and many more than you might imagine have made the very best of very little. This chapter looks at a vast array of options. It offers some practical advice – the inside gen from a make-up artist to the stars – and a 'Fashion In Music' quiz to test your knowledge of musical style icons that will provide further inspiration for your own 'Look'.

4. Determination

I bet every one of you has heard or read a story about the singer, writer, actor who got turned down so many times they were on the point of giving up, and then they finally got their lucky break. Well it's true, it's very, very difficult to achieve fame and fortune in the world of entertainment and you are going to have to weather an awful lot of knockbacks and disappointments.

In the fame game 'Determination' is inextricably linked with 'Self-Belief' but that's a bit more complicated which is why it gets a whole section of its own. Determination is a much more practical Fame Factor. It involves getting out there and doing things, knocking on doors, re-writing that song for the umpteenth time, practising for weeks on end in dismal, damp rehearsal rooms and, in fact, a lot of sheer hard work. This chapter asks you to assess how much you are truly willing to put yourself through to achieve your goal.

5. Stamina

You don't quite need the stamina to run a marathon to make it as a pop star but if you're intending to command an immense Arena stage for two hours a night, in six inch heels on a six month world tour, then you'd definitely better get yourself a serious fitness programme.

Even if you don't dance or run around the stage, you'll still need to know how to look after your vocal chords. Have you any idea how much it would cost you to give 15,000 people their money back and still pay all of the crew for each night of the tour you've had to cancel because you've lost your voice?

If you ask any pop star how many days off they had in the first two or three years of their career, you'll be horrified by the answer. This chapter takes a look at some gruelling actual itineraries and discovers just how much stamina an average pop star requires, before asking you to measure your own energy levels against them.

6. PR'ability

As a rising star you will need publicity and lots of it. You need 'PR'ability'; an engaging or quirky personality and something interesting to say that captures everyone's imagination because, surprise surprise, 'nice new star releases record' is never going to make the headlines.

However, this Fame Factor is also a whole minefield waiting to explode in your face if you don't approach it with caution and some expert advice. We analyse the headlines that worked alongside those that famously didn't. We decide whether a journalist can ever be your friend, whether there truly is no such thing as bad publicity and whether a famous PR was right to tell her client, "Don't read it! Measure it!"

We ask how on earth the biggest stars with the most column inches answer the same question over and over again and make it sound like it's the first time they've said it. Finally, you get to try out your own media skills as you create your ideal interview and have an opportunity to consider how prepared you are for today's media invasion of privacy.

7. Self-Belief

Clearly if you are going to stand up and perform in front of 20,000 or even maybe 150,000 people, you are going to need a large helping of 'Self-Belief' and that's exactly why this Fame Factor is probably the most fascinating. It's a weird quirk of nature that very often those same artists who can sell out an arena tour, are the same ones that are also wracked with personal self-doubt and need the affirmation of the audience's applause to feel good about themselves.

We look at the tipping point that allows an artist to get up on stage for the first time, to strike out on their own from a successful band, to keep turning up at those auditions despite constant rejections or to make it to the top only to crumble under the glare of constant media scrutiny. We also provide a quiz to test your own resolve and inner-strength, to see how you measure up on this fascinating scale.

8. Supporting cast

Scratch the surface of any truly successful star and you will find an impressive 'Supporting Cast' that might run into hundreds of people once you take into account the manager, agent, producer, record company, PA, driver, security, tour manager, tour promoter, tour production team, sound crew, lighting designer, set designers, stylists, make-up artists and choreographers.

This chapter explains what they all do and gives advice on the qualities you should look for in the team around you, especially in your manager and I talk to two of the best: Kylie's manager of twenty years, Terry Blamey, and Hilary Shaw who manages Girls Aloud.

Finally, if you become a member of a successful group then you and your band members will be each other's 'Supporting Cast' and the 'Solo or Spice Girl' quiz helps you to weigh up the advantages and disadvantages of sharing the limelight and whether you are likely to flourish best as part of a group or as a solo artist.

9. Killer Moves

Pop music is inextricably linked with dancing, always has been, always will be, whether it's the slickest Michael Jackson dance routine, a rave in an Ibiza night club or a night at G.A.Y. where every single person on the dance floor has Madonna's 'Vogue' choreography down to perfection. Therefore it's hardly surprising that Killer Moves is a crucial Fame Factor. Great dancing ability and choreography are clearly a massive asset to any performer and a pretty standard part of most pop artists' repertoires.

In this chapter I look at the most successful and effective movers and shakers since pop music began right up to those performing in the current charts. As well as interviewing a top choreographer, I look at the many ways that pop and rock icons have impressed their audiences with their moves, or lack of them, and help you to figure out what works best for you and how to prepare for a crucial audition. In short, it's all about stage presence – have you got it and if not, how can you get it?

10. Public Appeal

The revival and recent explosion of TV talent shows highlights this Fame Factor better than anything else as, to state the obvious, to win the competition you need the public to pick up the phone and vote for you, sometimes in their millions. But of course it doesn't end there because once the immediate blaze of publicity has died down, you have to keep on convincing the public to part with their hard cash to buy your records, merchandising and tickets for your show, just like every other artist out there.

Let's presume that you have the talent, the hit songs and all the other Fame Factors, this is probably the one that will ensure you have a career for years or, if you are really lucky, for decades. That is always assuming you can solve the conundrum of moving forward creatively without alienating your fans by changing too much or too quickly! This Fame Factor is a little trickier to pin down which is what makes it so interesting. We analyse the qualities that have made some of our biggest pop icons so appealing and see what you can learn from them.

THE FAME FACTOR STARS

At this point you could cheat and go straight to the end of the book to see how I scored my stars on the Fame Factor grid…

Or you could have a look at their mini CV's on these next few pages and decide who you think best embodies each of the Fame Factors and whether you agree with the stars I have awarded them. Of course there are so many more examples I could have chosen and there are lots of stories to tell; I'll reveal those as we go through the book.

You and your friends may not agree with my choices or even with each other, that's one of the joys of music. What is important is that you think about the qualities your favourite artists share with these Fame Factor icons and how you can best emulate them and their success.

Michael Jackson

The tragic news of Michael Jackson's death broke literally the day that I was due to deliver the first draft of this book to the publishers. Of course I held it back, thinking that I must check everything I had written in the light of the terribly sad news; I also spent the next two days talking to the dozens of interviewers who invariably call me up for a comment whenever anything momentous like this happens.

When I returned to my draft, there was in fact nothing that I wanted to change. Michael Jackson had always been my first choice of the perfect pop icon. I had already chosen to look past his increasingly bizarre later life, back to the young star who was having hits by the age of eleven with his brothers in the Jackson Five; the artist who went on to sell 750 million records worldwide and to record possibly the greatest, and certainly the most successful pop album of all time, 'Thriller'. Throughout the book he crops up time and time again as a perfect example for so many of my Fame Factors for his sheer creativity, originality and brilliance.

Girls Aloud

Girls Aloud started their career as the band voted together by the audience on 'Popstars The Rivals' and two of the members almost didn't make it to the final ten. However, they went on to kick start their career with the number one Christmas single and have become one of the most successful girl groups ever, with twenty consecutive top ten hits including three number ones and their first eight releases charting in the top five. They consistently make great pop records with: 'Sound of the Underground', 'I'll Stand By You', 'Something Kinda Ooooh', 'Love Machine' and 'Jump' to name but a few.

The girls continue to epitomise the glamorous life of a successful girl group and sell out arena tours. In between her commitments to the band, Cheryl Cole recently turned from 'poacher to gamekeeper' as she joined the X Factor panel alongside Simon Cowell and Louis Walsh, replacing Sharon Osborne.

Madonna

Madonna Louise Ciccone has been having hits for almost a quarter of a century. She has starred in movies, created controversy with some of her overtly provocative video performances and continues to be a brilliant dancer. She has been a style icon throughout her career and has created the most lavish and creative stage productions.

With hits like: 'Like A Virgin', 'Papa Don't Preach' and 'Vogue' through to 'Like A Prayer', 'True Blue', 'Ray of Light' and 'Hollywood'; she has sold over 200 million records worldwide.

Simon Cowell

In the past seven years Simon has moved from being a very rich and successful record company executive to becoming one of the richest and most famous men in the world with a guest appearance as himself on the Simpsons and an alleged declined invitation to dinner with Barack Obama due to a diary clash!

Simon was already responsible for millions of record sales with artists like Sinitta, Robson and Jerome and Westlife, when he decided to appear as a judge on the first series of Pop Idol and American Idol where he become instantly famous for his ruthless put downs.

His TV production company Syco then went on to create and produce the TV franchises for the 'X Factor', 'Britain's Got Talent' and 'America's Got Talent', earning Simon mega millions and international stardom along the way.

Lady Gaga

As this book goes to print Lady Gaga is a relatively recent arrival in the pop charts which makes it all the more remarkable that she has made such an impact in such a short time. She has moved swiftly from her early outrageous club performances and a musical style described as 'avant garde dance electronica', to securing a number one pop hit with 'Poker Face' all over the world!

However, since Lady Gaga's writing credits for other artists already include: Akon, Britney Spears, New Kids On The Block, Pussycat Dolls and Fergie; it is likely that her pedigree as a writer combined with her talent for self-publicity will ensure that she is going to be around for some time to come.

Leona Lewis

Leona Lewis captured the X Factor audience's hearts and votes and went on to have a massive hit in America with 'Bleeding Love'. The record made the number one spot there and in thirty other countries around the world.

She quickly signed a major recording deal in the States with music legend Clive Davis' J Records. Clive Davis was the man who signed and nurtured Whitney Houston and the deal was a joint venture between Clive and Simon Cowell; the first of its kind. Her debut album Spirit has sold six-and-a-half million copies worldwide at the time of going to print. Leona has won MOBO and MTV Awards and has been nominated for three Grammys.

Robbie Williams

If Robbie Williams' career had ended when Take That split up, he would already have had a fantastic career as a pop star with four Brit

Awards, eight number one singles including 'Pray', 'Never Forget' and 'Relight My Fire' and sales of over 19 million records.

However, Robbie chose to leave and strike out on his own and was soon crowing about his *eleven* solo Brit awards, more than any other artist! As a solo artist he has sold over 55 million records with anthemic hits like 'Angels' 'Let me Entertain You' and 'Millennium' and memorable collaborations like 'Kids' with Kylie Minogue and 'Somethin' Stupid' with Nicole Kidman.

Spice Girls

In 1993 five girls auditioned for a new pop band. It took three years for them to achieve their first hit 'Wannabe' but within a year it had become the most successful debut single ever, reaching number one in thirty-one countries including America. The hits, including 'Spice Up Your Life', 'Who Do You Think You Are' and 'Stop', kept flowing and made them the best selling British band since the Beatles.

'Girl Power', their first book, sold 200,000 copies on the first day of publication and was translated into more than twenty languages and their 'Spice World' movie was one of the most profitable films in the history of British cinema grossing £8.5 million in the UK and $30 million in America. Throughout their meteoric career they gathered acres of newspaper headlines but the most bizarre must surely have been Nelson Mandela's statement on meeting them: "These are my heroes. This is the greatest day of my life."

Kylie Minogue

Kylie is a rare creature. A pop star who has achieved continued success for more than two decades and a very special place in the hearts of her fans and the general public. She has sold over 60 million records and has had more than fifty international hit singles including: 'I Should Be So Lucky', 'Better The Devil You Know', 'Shocked', 'Can't Get You Out Of My Head' and 'On A Night Like This' which she performed to a TV audience of over four billion viewers at the spectacular closing ceremony of the Sydney Olympics.

Winning her first TV role at eleven, she was an award-winning actress in Australia long before she joined the cast of Neighbours. However 'Charlene' captured the hearts of every pre-teen girl (and lots of the boys) in Britain and catapulted her pop career into orbit.

An actress, singer and dancer, her shows have become increasingly more spectacular; she has won countless awards including an OBE and she has probably sold more glossy magazines by gracing their covers with stunning photos than any other single star. Madame Tussauds, the famous waxworks museum in London, currently displays their fourth version of Kylie (only the Queen has more models made).

Beyoncé Knowles

As a member of Destiny's Child and then as a solo artist Beyoncé Knowles has sold over 75 million records including; 'Say My Name', 'Survivor', 'Single Ladies (Put A Ring On It)', 'If I Were A Boy' and 'Crazy In Love'. In 2001 she won Songwriter of the Year, awarded by the American Society of Composers, Authors and Publishers, and became the first African American female and the second female songwriter of all time to gain this honour.

She has also starred in several major movies, in particular 'Dreamgirls' in which she played the Diana Ross inspired role and for which she was nominated for two Golden Globe awards. She is sexy, beautiful and a fantastic dancer with an amazing voice; attributes that her stage alter ego Sasha Fierce exploits to maximum effect.

My CV...

I've been passionate about music all my life and along the way I've been lucky enough (some might even say 'lucky, lucky, lucky'!) to work with some of the greatest talents and most successful pop stars in the world including Michael Jackson, Elton John and the Beatles. I've been single-minded, determined, never short of an opinion and I've also worked incredibly hard.

As a DJ in the 60's I sought out the records that would instantly fill a dance floor. I admired and one day hoped to emulate the greatest Hit Factory in the world, Tamla Motown, home to the Jackson Five, The Supremes and Marvin Gaye. Later on I worked in America where I met Berry Gordy, Motown's founder. I was so impressed by the way his brilliant team prepared and polished their young stars for future fame, pairing them with the best producers and songwriters. I watched and I learned.

In the 70's I started producing my own hit records and in the 80's I would use all of that crucial knowledge to build my own PWL Hit Factory (and where incidentally Simon Cowell would stalk me until I agreed to work with his artists). At PWL I used the skills I had learnt to launch the careers of many young artists, achieving fame and pop stardom for artists such as Steps, Rick Astley, Jason Donovan and Kylie Minogue.

In the 80's Stock Aitken Waterman clocked up over 120 top 20 hits as writers and producers, including 17 number ones and for several years in the 80's hardly a week went by when we didn't have a top 10 record in the chart. Of course along the way we also made some mistakes, from which I learnt even more about what you need to be a success.

So, as I look at the ten crucial elements that make-up the Fame Factor, I'll also be sharing some of my own experiences, both good and bad; experiences that helped to hone my instincts for spotting not just talent but the whole package – in other words, the Fame Factor.

And by breaking that elusive Fame Factor down into its 10 crucial elements you can decide for yourself whether you truly have what it takes to be a star.

FAME FACTOR I

THE SONGS

Let's start by stating the obvious; to be a successful pop star you need hit songs and lots of them. So it's not surprising that my first Fame Factor, and in fact the only one you simply cannot do without, 'The Songs'. Slightly more surprising is the fact that it's also the one Fame Factor that so many pop stars, even some of my pop icons, are missing; of course they all have brilliant records, but only a few are also brilliant songwriters.

Take another look at my list of pop icons – did you figure out which one I was going to highlight as the perfect example of the pop star with the stunning songs? Perhaps the question should be how many of them have actually written their own hit singles? Well I can tell you; only half of them.

Writing a hit song is very difficult; if it was easy everyone would be doing it! In this chapter I talk about what makes a classic hit record, how vastly different they can be and some things to think about if you intend to write your own material. We'll also look at what you can do if you don't happen to have the song writing genius of Michael Jackson.

This chapter also includes a pocket biography that will shed some light on how I got to be so opinionated and how I learnt what makes a hit record, although to be fair I was probably just as opinionated at the start! I have always been passionate about hit songs and it has never, ever ceased to amaze me the number of people who would pitch up at my office with a demo tape, or perform one of their own songs at a Pop Idol audition, when the song was truly dreadful. Self-delusion and self-belief lie dangerously close to one another, and we'll look at that in more detail later in this book.

Michael Jackson – song writing genius…

For me Michael Jackson is indeed the pop icon who would score a Fame Factor of 11 out of 10 for 'The Songs' every time; and as I said at the start, his early demise did nothing to add to or detract from my admiration for him as an artist. By the age of eleven he was fronting the Jackson Five and performing classic pop hits like 'ABC' and 'I Want You Back' written for them by Tamla Motown's amazing stable of writers. He was getting the best musical education in the world and learning song writing lesson number one:

A hit song needs a memorable 'hook'

Michael decided to go solo, however, with 'Off The Wall' he was still learning his craft as a songwriter and cleverly collaborated with some amazing writers including Paul McCartney, Stevie Wonder and Rod Temperton. He also moved from the brilliant, if rather formulaic, Tamla Motown producers to work with Quincy Jones, the musical genius who was hugely instrumental in helping Michael find his own distinctive sound. He had already built on lesson number two:

Always work with the best available co-writers and producers

By his early thirties Michael Jackson had written some of the greatest and most original pop songs of all time, classics like: 'Wanna Be Startin' Somethin'', 'Beat It', 'Don't Stop Till You get Enough', 'Billie Jean', 'Bad', 'Black Or White', 'I Just Can't Stop Loving You', 'The Way You Make Me Feel' and had become the biggest selling artist of all time. All of his songs also illustrate lesson number three:

The lyrics must capture the listeners' imagination or emotion or both

There's a very good reason that around 90% of all great songs are about love, but there are hundreds of great songs about different things that matter to people. We'll look at some of them later but first I'm going to tell you a bit about ten of my favourite records. The reasons I chose them illustrate that song writing is a complex art and that although the rules above will always apply there are also many different ways to create a hit song. And if we're talking about a hit record, which is of course the point here, then the production is also vital, and for me you can't separate one from the other.

10 OF PETE'S FAVOURITE SONGS...

1. Heard It Through The Grapevine – Marvin Gaye
The most brilliant and heartbreaking song about betrayal. If the love of your life is cheating on you, what's the worst way you could possibly find out about it? It must surely be to hear it from someone else. The record is the perfect marriage of a faultless lyric and musical arrangement with Marvin Gaye's soulful vocals. The bass riff intro to this song is the one that makes the hairs stand up on the back of my neck every single time I hear it.

2. Common People – Pulp
I first heard this record on a Top 40 chart run down show. I liked the tune and the hook straightaway and took it at first for a humourous piece of pop confection. Then Jarvis Cocker's lyric really intrigued me as he had cleverly wrapped up some fairly hard hitting social comment within the framework of a story about a boy who tries to impress a girl he meets at college but just can't stop himself from pointing out how stupid her belief is that 'common people are cool'.

3. The Locomotion – Little Eva
In some ways this is a novelty record, a silly little song about a new dance craze but with a great vocal and melody. However, novelty records can also sometimes pull an unsuspecting listener into music the way a more serious record might not. Finding Little Eva led me to the Shirelles and their 'Will You Still Love Me Tomorrow', and in one move I had been drawn from a little novelty record into a lifelong love affair with the song's writer, Carole King, one of the greatest songwriters in the world.

4. The Winner Takes It All – Abba
This record and Abba's performance of it awes me every single time I hear it. Singing the stunning melody, Agnetha (the blonde one) tells a tale of bitter heartbreak and divorce. It's a universal tale that so many people can identify with, but the thing that amazes me about her passionate

performance is that the song was recorded immediately after the break-up of her own marriage to fellow Abba member, Bjorn Ulvaeus, who also wrote and produced the song and performed it with her on stage.

5. Let's Dance – David Bowie
On first acquaintance you might think this quite a simple song, and for a wordsmith as talented as David Bowie the lyrics are certainly repetitive; but this song is a perfect combination of what was then state-of-the-art production technology and simplicity. I talk about a lyric needing to connect with its audience and this record does this in an entirely physical way; Bowie sings 'Let's Dance' and we do!

6. Visions – Stevie Wonder
Stevie Wonder has dozens of classic songs but I picked 'Visions' for its haunting melody, because the record creates an other-worldly mood and because sometimes a lyric just touches you in a way that's hard to explain. When Stevie Wonder talks, as a blind man, about the leaves turning from green to brown and asks us to look at the visions in our minds, I find it a total inspiration.

7. God Only Knows – The Beach Boys
If a songwriter is lucky, once or twice in their lives, and often at their highest or lowest points, they will create a real gem. With 'God Only Knows' Brian Wilson takes a title that is familiar before you even hear the gorgeous but fairly simple basic melody, and adds the exquisite harmonies. For me this is a song about recognition and another universal emotion, 'God only knows what I'd be without you'.

8. With A Song In My Heart – Ella Fitzgerald
If you're over fifty you'll recognise this melody as the theme tune for the long running BBC radio request show, 'Two Way Family Favourites' and I include it as a great pop song partly to remind people that not all pop songs were written after 1960. True, it is has an unashamedly sentimental and schmaltzy lyric, but the intensity of Ella Fitzgerald's performance converts it into a classic poetic love song.

9. Kid Charlemagne - Steely Dan

We're going to talk about lyrics a lot more in a moment but here's a classic example of not taking the obvious route as Steely Dan deliver a treatise on the history and effects of the drug LSD and the men who first experimented with it. Add to this their trademark intricate and luscious layered sound and one of the greatest guitar solos ever recorded and you have a truly great record.

10. She Loves You – The Beatles

For me this is the best and most effective love story ever told. It is passionate, truthful and it gets straight to the point delivering its story in a perfect two and a half minute pop song.

It took me twenty years to become an overnight sensation

For the past twenty years or so my ability to pick a hit song has been instinctive; yes I may have started out with some innate talent but that instinct is based on an encyclopaedic knowledge of music. My theme throughout this chapter is not to tell you exactly how to write a hit song; I do believe it requires an element of god-given talent. Instead I want you to go away and really listen to, and analyse, a whole load of successful songs and decide whether you can really compete with them.

If you can't you're in good company with a lot of very successful pop stars and we'll see how they get around this a bit later. But first let's go back for a moment to the basics and the question that everyone always asks me – how do *I* know when it's a hit song? I promised you a pocket biography so here it is: my route to success and the lessons I learnt along the way.

Over the past four decades I have been involved with over 500 hit records. I have promoted them, written and produced them, published them or released them on the PWL label; but forty years ago it started like this...

Just like you I started out as a music fan, in the truest sense of the word, I was actually a music fanatic. I began my music career as a DJ playing records in the Midlands dance halls; it was the 60's and the Beatles were still a new Beat group performing package tours under the banner of the Mersey Sound. It's going to be hard for most of you to imagine a time when it was difficult to hear pop or rock music on the radio so hearing it played at your local Mecca ballroom on a Saturday night was really exciting. This is several decades before mixing and scratching were even a twinkle in the eye of the cult of DJ's that rose to prominence in the 90's.

What I'm talking about here is 7" vinyl pop hits and the acid test for a new record was whether or not it filled the dance floor. In those days my job as a DJ depended on my manager seeing exactly that at every possible opportunity; it was a crucial lesson in my musical education. I learnt very quickly what worked and the stone bonk certainties were the American imports on the Tamla Motown record label.

By the 70's I was also promoting records at radio stations. Once again my reputation depended on knowing when to really push a record with the radio producers. Now instead of feet on the dance floor, the radio stations were chasing listeners, once again it was all about getting it right with the public. I also worked in the States with Philadelphia International, their legendary writers Gamble and Huff and arranger Thom Bell. While there I met one of my all time heroes Berry Gordy; I would later base the PWL Hit Factory on his incredibly successful Motown model.

In the 80's I crossed over fully into the record and music publishing business. I became an A&R manager, first for Elton's Rocket Records and then for Magnet Records. People often ask what A&R stands for and when you tell them 'Artists and Repertoire' they look slightly blank. It dates back to the first days of the record labels and quite simply means finding and signing the talented artists and then finding the repertoire, or songs, for them to sing. For the A&R men and women of many of today's pop stars this is still the same role.

Once again my reputation and salary depended on getting it right with the public and luckily we had some early success with The Lambrettas at Rocket and Alvin Stardust and Chris Rea at Magnet.

By now I had decided that I knew what the public wanted and I wanted to make my own records; the next step was to team up with a brilliant producer, Peter Collins. We produced hits for Musical Youth, Match Box, Alvin Stardust and Nik Kershaw.

We also started working for Dave Robinson, the mad genius who started the legendary Stiff Records, producing hits for Tracey Ullman and the Belle Stars. 'Robbo', who for some unknown reason always called me 'Watermax', was a brilliantly instinctive marketing man but he was backed up by Paul Conroy from whom I also learnt a huge amount and who went on to be a crucial factor in the Spice Girls' success. Peter Collins and I eventually parted amicably and he went to live and work in America where he chalked up huge success with major rock acts including Bon Jovi.

Around this time I met Mike Stock and Matt Aitken, two jobbing songwriters who had yet to have a hit record, and the rest, as they say, is history. I put everything I'd learnt so far and all of my money into building the PWL studios and label, and together Stock Aitken Waterman amassed over a hundred hit singles and albums for ourselves and other record labels, including of course several for my good friend Simon Cowell. We still hold the distinction of being the only writers to have won 'Best Songwriters of the Year' for three consecutive years. Our biggest selling artists included Kylie, Jason Donovan, Dead or Alive, Rick Astley, Sinitta and Bananarama.

So now that I've reminded you of my pop credentials, let's take a closer look at one of the crucial elements for a great song.

Lyrics –
'The world has had enough of silly love songs'…

Paul McCartney suggested this in his song of the same name and then immediately said it 'wasn't so', and as I mentioned earlier, probably 90% of hits are written about love – longing for love, finding love and losing love. But there are also fabulous examples of brilliant songs whose lyrics had nothing to do with love and probably helped them to stand out from the crowd in the first place.

Think about Band Aid and 'Do They Know It's Christmas', a song about banishing poverty in Ethiopia, or 'Bohemian Rhapsody' Queen's operatic stream of consciousness asking if Scaramouche can do the fandango!

We've got it covered...

Still not sure you're going to make it as a song writer? Well, if so few pop stars are also brilliant writers where do they get their hit songs from? They do one of three things; they either co-write with a great writer, have great songs written for them by professional writers, or they use the time-honoured route of recording a cover version of an existing hit.

'Covering' a song is a publishing term and in this context it applies to an artist recording or 'covering' a song written by someone else and in common parlance the word cover generally refers to a song that has already been a hit for another artist.

The reason that record companies love covers is that the song has already been tried out on the public and has a proven track record. However, the skill is in picking the right song to cover.

Louis Walsh and their respective record companies have made Westlife and Boyzone a fortune with an incredibly successful selection of covers:

Boyzone –   Father and Son – original by Cat Stevens
             Love Me For A Reason – original by The Osmonds
             When the Going Gets Tough – original by Billy Ocean
             Words – original by The Bee Gees

Westlife –   Mandy – original by Barry Manilow
             Uptown Girl – original by Billy Joel
             I Have a Dream – original by Abba
             The Rose – original by Bette Midler

NAME THAT TUNE

Can you identify the following songs from the description of their lyrics; they are all massive hits. (Answers on page 35)

1. Elton John sings a tribute to screen goddess Marilyn Monroe

2. Girls Aloud sing about the dance sounds that get them going on the dance floor

3. Don MacLean sings a surreal story about the day that Buddy Holly died

4. The Kaiser Chiefs sing about trouble brewing on the streets of Leeds

5. Madonna sings about telling her father's she's pregnant

6. Georgie Fame sings about the rise and fall of two notorious bank robbers

7. The Jam sing about a fight with the young 'toffs' at a public school

8. David Bowie sings about the life as an astronaut and the attendant dangers

9. The Beatles sing about a street in their home town of Liverpool

10. Michael Jackson sings about horror movies

My Top Tips for finding covers

1. Step Back In Time

With Mike Stock and Matt Aitken at PWL I had the luck to be working with two fantastic songwriters but we still had some massive successes with covers which we tended to pick from several decades earlier so that our target market wouldn't necessarily be aware of the original, and then re-record them with modern production values. You may recognise these hits but did you know who recorded the originals?

Kylie

The Locomotion	Little Eva – 1962
Tears on My Pillow	Little Antony & the Imperials–1958

Jason Donovan

Sealed With A Kiss	Bryan Hyland – 1962

Bananarama

Venus	Shocking Blue – 1969

2. Steer clear of the obvious; the more unexpected the cover the better, but it has to be an amazing song in the first place

'Hallelujah' – Simon Cowell gave his new pop princess Alexandra Burke a song by the dark and poetic Leonard Cohen, (though I still prefer Rufus Wainwright's version).

'The Star Spangled Banner' – many patriots thought Jimi Hendrix's interpretation of the America national anthem was tantamount to treason.

'God Save The Queen' – HRH is still wondering why the Sex Pistols are not locked up in the Tower.

Sinatra fans felt the same way about Syd Vicious's version of 'My Way'.

3. Take a song originally recorded in one genre and record it in another

'You Were Always On My Mind' – Elvis Presley
The Pet Shop Boys added a techno beat to the Elvis Classic.

'Comfortably Numb' – Pink Floyd
Scissor Sisters inspired techno version of the druggy rock anthem.

'I Just Don't Know What To Do With Myself' – Dusty Springfield
The White Stripes pared the lush production back the raw emotion of the lyrics.

'Tainted Love' – Gloria Jones
Soft Cell turned an R'n'B classic into an electro pop gay anthem.

'Nothing Compares To You' – Prince
Sinead O' Connor's haunting version of a less well-known song by the Purple One

'All Along The Watch Tower' – Bob Dylan
Jimi Hendrix added heavy electric guitar riffs to a folk song.

4. Mixing it up…

Here's another sub section which mixes up the genres and includes the hook from a cover or an original hit record (note you will need the original artist and publisher's permission to do this).

'Walk This Way' - Run DMC and Aerosmith
'Gold Digger' -   Kanye West's signature record with Jamie Foxx
                  singing Ray Charles 'I Got A Woman'

'Umbrella' - Rihanna featuring Jay-Z

I've read all the advice and I'm going to write myself a hit...

So if you believe you have the talent to write your own songs and have taken on board the advice in this chapter, then go for it – you may be the next Lady Gaga. However, at the end of this book, when you have weighed up everything that goes with being a successful pop star, you might just decide that you have a special writing talent and you'd be just as happy in the background, writing and producing songs for successful artists. It's no easier to get into this position, but speaking personally it's a fantastically fulfilling life and can clearly also be a very lucrative one.

To succeed on either of these routes, first you need a great demo. These days you can do this yourself at home on the computer or rope in some musician friends to help. Whether you want to record the song professionally yourself or have it covered by someone else, this is the time to try to secure a publishing deal with a pro-active publisher (see also Fame Factor 8 – Supporting Cast), who recognises your talent and will then punt your songs out to the A&R managers, artist managers and record producers.

The publisher will know what type of artists and songs the record companies are looking for. The publisher may also pay for the songs to be demoed to a higher standard than you could achieve at home and might add session singers who can perform the songs in the style of the artist they are being pitched to.

P. S.

If you are the songwriter for the band, your fellow band members will love you for providing the hits – right up to the moment that the first publishing royalties arrive and you suddenly become considerably richer than the rest of them! (Reportedly one of the main reasons for Take That's first demise, as Gary Barlow was and remains by far the best songwriter in the group!)

Getting in the Professionals...

If you are really lucky your record company or manager will commission one of the song writing elite; a relatively small group of song writers who are responsible for a huge cache of perfect pop songs tailor made for the most promising or most successful pop stars. It was always so; if you look back to the golden days of Tamla Motown, The Jackson Five, the Four Tops and The Supremes all had songs written for them, often by Motown's famous production and song writing team, Holland Dozier Holland.

Guy Chambers and Cathy Dennis are just two of the leading writers in this field. Guy is the co-writer with Robbie Williams on: 'Let Me Entertain You', 'Angels', 'Kids' (Robbie's duet with Kylie). Cathy's credits include: 'Toxic' for Britney, 'Never Had A Dream Come True' for S Club 7, 'I Kissed A Girl' for Katy Perry and 'Can't Get you Out Of My Head' for Kylie.

I've talked about SAW's incredible run of hits and I've told this story many times before but for those of you that haven't heard it – this is the story of the first song we ever wrote for Kylie. Mushroom records had signed her in Australia and had asked us to write a song for her. As I mentioned earlier we were a bit busy in the late 80's and I had actually forgotten that it was the day 'Charlene' from Neighbours was due to come into the studio to record her first single written specially by us for her.

Kylie was waiting in the missile room – our waiting room at the studio, so called because it had an exocet missile hanging from the ceiling (I was going through a phase of collecting military memorabilia). I went through to the studio and broke the news to Mike (Stock) and Matt (Aitken) that I'd forgotten to mention to them that Kylie was coming in. We were used to working to ridiculous schedules and under pressure but when I told them we only had her for the day Mike looked at me and snorted "she should be so lucky!" and the rest as they say…

Stuff That You Can Do…

1. Listen to music

Of course you do already, but I mean *really* listen to all kinds of music especially those songs that have been massive hits and try to work out why.

2. Test your song's staying power

The Old Grey Whistle Test was a cult music TV that started in 1971 and in many ways the title was an ironic misnomer since the 'old grey whistle test' referred to songs that were instantly memorable and the TV programme showcased more eclectic, progressive music. The term comes from the era when Tin Pan Alley was the centre of music publishing and writers would test their new songs on the 'old greys', the doormen in grey suits. If they could remember it after just one listen, the song was deemed worth pursuing.

I'm not asking you to go and find a load of old men in grey suits and try your songs out on them, but rather look at the list of the best selling singles of all time. In 90% of cases most people will be able to sing the hook from the title of the record which emphasises another of my pet hobby horses. If you want someone to remember your song from the title, it had better also be the record's hook!

3. Learn an instrument

There are some great pop songwriters and lyricists who don't play an instrument but they are in the minority.

4. Master a basic music production programme on your computer

Once you've bought the basic kit you could save yourself hundreds of pounds in demo studio fees, and you can record every day if you need to.

5. Get a Dictaphone

And keep it with you at all times, including when you are asleep – you'd be amazed how many ideas have come to me in the middle of the night and if you don't record them, they will float off into the ether never to be seen or heard again

6. Find an obscure cover

By raiding your parents' (and grandparents') music record collection

Answers to the 'name that tune' quiz

1. Candle In The Wind – Bernie Taupin later adapted the lyrics for a tribute to Princess Diana that Elton performed at her funeral

2. Sound of the Underground – the girls' first hit and a Christmas number one

3. American Pie – the original single was unusual in that it was around 8 minutes long and continued on the B side of the record

4. I Predict A Riot – the band's signature hit which must surely be the only modern hit to include the line 'I tell thee'; Yorkshire dialect and the archaic form of 'you'

5. Papa Don't Preach – the singer tells her father she's keeping her illegitimate baby

6. The Ballad of Bonnie and Clyde – two American gangsters whose story was somewhat glamourised by the film in which they were played by Faye Dunaway and Warren Beatty

7. Eton Rifles – Eton is the public school traditionally frequented by the sons of the landed gentry

8. Space Oddity – with its famous line 'Ground Control to Major Tom', this classic was released to coincide with the Apollo moon landings

9. Penny Lane paints a snapshot of the people in Penny Lane going about their daily business

10. Thriller – and the video came complete with zombies

A DISTINCTIVE VOICE

Over the years I have worked with plenty of brilliant singers who have incredible ranges and can sing in almost any style. They've appeared on hundreds of top 10 records; yet very few have had any real success in their own right. How can this be?

It's because they are a select band of what we call in the business 'session' singers as they are booked by the three hour session to provide backing vocals: in the studio, sometimes on tour and occasionally to prop up a dodgy lead vocal.

The truth is that they often sing better than the stars whose records they appear on, but they don't have a 'Distinctive Voice' which is why they work so well in the background but are rarely asked to sing lead vocal.

So let's get this straight; I'm not saying you don't need a brilliant voice. I'm not saying that having an impressive range, or the ability to deliver complicated vocal gymnastics isn't an advantage; what I am saying is that you can have all of those things but what you really need is a *distinctive* voice.

I'll go further and say that your voice may not even appeal to everybody but your fans will love it and even those who don't love it will recognise it instantly as soon as they hear one of your records. My pop star icon who embodies this Fame Factor is Madonna because whether the record is perfect pop like 'Holiday', an iconic classic like 'Vogue or the dance hit 'Ray of Light', you know immediately that it's Madonna.

I will admit here and now that I don't actually love the tone of her voice and this clearly doesn't matter one jot since she's had countless hits, has sold over two hundred million records worldwide and is one of the most enduring pop stars with a legion of devoted fans. Incidentally I also think that she scores full marks on all of the Fame Factor elements.

Take a look at my list of icons and see how many have the same kind of instant vocal recognition. I suggest that the correlation between the distinctiveness of their voice and their success ratio will be very close.

The voices that stand out from the crowd...

By now you'll be expecting me to have opinions about the voices that best illustrate this Fame Factor (or contradict it!). So here are 10 examples of voices that I find either instantly recognisable or, in my opinion, have yet to stand the test of time. Take note of the little biographical notes on the backgrounds and influences that shaped their voices; we'll be coming back to that shortly.

1. Michael Jackson

Here was an artist with a brilliant AND a distinctive voice. He sang (and spoke) in a range much higher than most male singers, which is symptomatic of his whole persona; the boy who never grew up. He had a clarity to his delivery that was constant whether he was hammering out a staccato dance tune or crooning a sentimental ballad.

Michael was performing on stage from the age of eleven and to qualify to join his older brothers he had to master the art of dancing very young while and singing in close harmony.

2. Mariah Carey

Mariah obviously has an incredible voice, with an almost operatic range and control, which is less surprising when you consider that she reputedly started singing at the age of three encouraged by her mother who was a former opera singer and vocal coach. Her precocious ability won her work as a studio session singer while she was still at school.

I loved her voice on early records like 'Vision of Love' and 'Hero' but for me she has a tendency to indulge her temptation to show off by adding too many 'trills' – singing up and down the scale before arriving at the actual note. Lots of singers do this and there's a fine line between adding colour to the vocal and going overboard and spoiling a great melody.

3. Whitney Houston

Whitney's vocal on 'I Will Always Love You' is the perfect illustration for me of a singer adding just enough vocal gymnastics to add drama and pathos without distracting from the gorgeous melody and lyric. Whenever you hear 'I Wanna Dance With Somebody' or 'Saving All My Love for You', it can only be one singer – Whitney Houston. (Incidentally 'I Will Always Love You' was originally written and recorded by Dolly Parton and if you listen to them back to back they illustrate perfectly my point in the previous chapter about finding the right song to cover. It's a fantastic song but Whitney's recording is the one that makes it a classic hit.)

Whitney has a very privileged musical background. She grew up surrounded by great voices. Her mother is soul singer Cissy Houston, Dionne Warwick is her cousin and her godmother is Aretha Franklin. She started singing in a junior gospel choir before progressing to singing alongside her mother in night clubs, which is where she was discovered.

4. Leona Lewis

Leona clearly has a fantastic voice which the public loved enough to vote her an X Factor winner. She's already had a massive hit in the States with 'Bleeding Love' but for me the jury is out on whether she has a truly 'Distinctive Voice'. It's perfect for a Saturday night Entertainment show but I'm not sure whether it is distinctive enough to sustain a high profile career.

Leona had a text book musical education, developing her vocal technique at the Sylvia Young Theatre School and the Italia Conti Academy before finally graduating from the BRIT school.

5. Will Young

Will has gone from being the plucky winner of a TV talent show, Pop Idol 2002, to becoming an established artist in his own right and for me that's all down to his 'Distinctive Voice'. The thing about Will is that he knows exactly how to use his voice to its best advantage by picking or writing the material that really suits it.

Will studied Musical Theatre at the Arts Educational School in Chiswick, London.

6. George Michael

When the remaining members of Queen decided to stage a tribute concert for Freddie Mercury, they gave themselves a bit of a dilemma. Everyone, it seemed, had slightly underrated his power and range, and in my view only one artist really showed that he had the vocal chords to match Freddie's and that was George Michael with his version of 'Somebody To Love'.

Like Madonna, George has written and performed so many different types of hit record; but from the pure pop 'Club Tropicana' to the emotional 'Jesus To A Child', the vocal is always and instantly identifiable as George Michael. Incidentally there are few other artists who could hold their own with soul diva Aretha Franklin but George did exactly that when he duetted with her on 'Knew You Were Waiting'.

George met his partner in Wham, Andrew Ridgeley, at school, before starting a band and writing songs. He was signed to CBS via a small label called Innervision Records and their second single 'Young Guns Go For It' was a top 10 hit.

7. Amy Winehouse

Here's another voice that I'm not completely mad about which isn't helped by Amy's more recent performances where she takes the jazz technique of sliding almost off the note to extremes. But there's no getting away from the fact that when you hear Amy on the radio, you immediately now it's her.

Interestingly she is also an ex-pupil of The Sylvia Young Theatre School and the BRIT school, although she was expelled from the former. Amy's route to success was via the traditional method of writing her own music and getting a tape to the right A&R person.

8. Rick Astley

Rick has a fantastic deep, warm rich baritone voice which is sensational but surprisingly difficult to record well. (I won't bore you with the full technicalities but it's to do with limiting the volume whilst retaining the depth and quality.) This is another totally memorable voice but one with a twist.

When Rick's first record 'Whenever You Need Somebody' was released in the America, everyone thought he was a big black American soul singer so the record created a double-whammy impact when he turned out to be a young white lad from Lancashire.

I spotted Rick when his manager dragged me to see him performing in a dodgy northern club, and while we experimented with writing the right song for him, he worked as the tea boy at PWL.

9. Lily Allen

Lily Allen's 'Mockney' delivery and a lyrical style that squeezes almost more words into each line than it can possibly take, make her voice instantly recognisable. Her vocal delivery is a great example of someone who has found a distinctive style that works for her and incidentally belies an education that includes some very swanky private schools.

Depending on which interview you read Lily either credits or discredits the advantage of having a famous actor/comedian for a father when looking for a record deal. Lily's whole persona is streetwise with a penchant to shock, but despite having attended thirteen schools, she also managed to achieve a grade eight singing qualification and found time to master piano, trumpet, violin and guitar.

10. Kylie

As soon as Kylie walked into the studio that very first time, (after we had written 'I Should Be So Lucky' at record speed!) we knew we had a superb voice to record. She had been a successful actress from the age of eleven, so as she matured from a pretty young girl full of youthful exuberance into a sexy young woman we were able to unfold a more sophisticated set of stories for her to tell, like 'Better The Devil' and 'Shocked'.

Kylie retained her vocal clarity and distinctive voice but used her acting skills to interpret each song individually.

And finally the stars of the Boy Bands

Let's be honest not all of the boys in any given boy band will have been chosen solely for their vocal abilities but here I'm looking at the ones that shine through.

That wasn't intended as a punning reference to Gary Barlow and Take That but it's an interesting case in point as Gary has a good and recognisable voice, retaining a slight Mancunian twang, but **Robbie Williams**' voice is totally distinctive and a huge factor in his solo success.

Robbie was only fifteen when he joined Take That but he had grown up watching his dad perform in the clubs.

Justin Timberlake who, like Britney and Christina Aguilera started his career as a child actor in Disney Channel's Mickey Mouse club, used his distinctive voice and songs like 'Cry Me A River' and 'Sexy Back' to move from huge success with NSYNC to even bigger solo acclaim.

Meanwhile **Westlife**, who truly do boast great singers, retain a trademark Irish lilt to their close harmonies. I could go on forever and have picked lots of different examples but my point is this – if you want to be a massive pop icon, this Fame Factor, 'Distinctive Voice' is a must-have; so what can you do to get one?

Well before you can get to distinctive, you must first have a good voice that is strong enough to work live and record well in the studio. There are all kinds of technical trickery that can be employed to assist a weaker voice but the basic kit should be there in the first place.

The route to a Distinctive Voice – things that you can do...

I have chosen some of the most distinctive voices ever so let's look at the routes they took to hone those skills and then get noticed and see how you might apply the lessons they learned.

1. Learn from your family
(Mariah, Whitney, Robbie)

OK, I accept that this is tricky if you don't happen to have a mother who was operatically trained or is a brilliant soul singer, but there are two things to take from this route. a) Even if it's not your immediate family there will be someone close to you, it may be a teacher who will want to help and encourage you if you have the beginnings of a voice. And b) remember that all three artists far outstripped their parents achievements.

2. Start young
(Michael Jackson, Mariah, Robbie, Kylie)
I wouldn't necessarily recommend that you join a professional group at 15 as Robbie did with Take That, but it's certainly never too young to start singing and if you're reading this with a dream of becoming a singer – just start now – and if you can't afford lessons, sing along with every record on the radio.

3. Get some professional training
(Will Young, Amy Winehouse, Leona Lewis)
As you can see, attending a theatre school does not necessarily result in you becoming a 'stage school kid'. You may not be able to afford the fees – most families can't but there are grants and bursaries and there are also loads of local weekend and evening classes you can attend.

4. Join a choir
(Whitney, Beyonce, Lily Allen)
Just because it's a cliché doesn't mean it isn't true that so many singers got their first experience of performing in a gospel choir. Singing in a choir can give you confidence in your voice and will definitely stretch you and give you new musical challenges; Lily Allen was apparently even a member of a chamber choir.

5. Learn to sing at the same time as dancing and harmonising
(Michael Jackson, Robbie Williams)
OK, so you can't expect to walk into the Jackson Five and get lessons from your big brothers but you can practice with your mates. Get hold of some old Backstreet Boys or Bananarama videos and see if you can recreate their performances with them.

6. Get yourself some singing lessons
(Lily Allen, Will Young, Amy Winehouse)

You don't want to end up sounding like you just graduated from stage school but then none of these artists did and it will be incredibly helpful to know about breathing, control and vocal exercises. The trick is to keep listening to, and trying to write, the music you are interested in, while making sure you have some skills to help you to find a distinctive sound of your own.

7. Make a demo tape and bring it to the attention
of an A&R manager
(Lily Allen, Amy Winehouse, George Michael)

Actually you may need to make several demo tapes until you have one on which you really like the sound of your voice, so get cracking as quickly as possible at recording and playing back your voice, experimenting with sounds.

8. Get some gigs, get a manager and perform live
(Rick Astley)

And if the manager's any good he'll drag a pop guru to see you play or at least some A&R Managers!

9. Become a successful child actor
(Kylie, Britney, Justin Timberlake)

OK, it's as tall an order as is becoming a pop star in the first place, but what you can take from this is that acting skills will give you invaluable voice control and the ability to really tell a story through the lyrics. It's a well known fact that lots of actors can sing and far less singers can act – get yourself this set of skills and you'll have a distinct advantage. Join the school or local drama group.

And finally...

I will finish with just two overriding pieces of advice for you to consider in your quest

★ Look after your voice – it's a muscle that needs stretching and exercising like any other.
★ Develop your own style – take inspiration from the wealth of music around you and then work on a voice that is distinctly you.

THE LOOK

Let's not beat about the bush here. Your chances of becoming a successful pop star are greatly enhanced if you are attractive and have Fame Factor 3 – The Look. I don't make the rules, I can't affect what the public likes to see on their screens, I'm not saying I think it's right, it's just a hard fact.

There are hundreds of books and magazines devoted to enhancing or disguising the attributes that nature gave you via diet, styling, make-up, hair and exercise so I'm not even going to attempt to go there in this book. What I will do, however, is to talk about the general principals, to explore some of 'The Looks' that have been a marketing man's dream and to talk to a professional who creates perfect pop star 'Looks'.

However, let's start from the basic premise that if you want to be a pop star (and I'm talking very specifically pop here); you've got to do as much for yourself as possible, and I don't mean major plastic surgery and extreme diets. If you starve yourself to anorexic proportions it will only play havoc with your skin and energy levels. I'm talking about eating a healthy balanced diet, canning the chips and greasy beef burgers and getting into shape. Yes, you can airbrush spots out of photos and carve inches off thighs but it's expensive and the record company would prefer to start with basic material (that's you) that is going to photograph well without all of that.

All I'm saying is that if you want to be a professional pop star it starts with taking a professional attitude to your own body, then you get to the fun bit, finding your 'Look' and deciding exactly what image you want to portray. This may be the point when you break out into a cold sweat; how on earth do you know what that is? In this chapter we break down the options to help you decide and start by asking…

What your 'Look' should do for you…

Like so many of the Fame Factors, 'The Look' is all about getting you noticed in the first place and then getting the public to remember you, to like you, fancy you, admire you and identify with you (check out what the fans are wearing at any major concert!). The right image for you can achieve some, most, or all of these things and we're going to break the possibilities down into some basic categories to help you to focus on the best one for you.

If you get it right you'll be helping the record company to market you and convincing them that the whole 'package' works. However, the record company may have very strong and opposing ideas as to what your image should be – listen to them, they are the experts, decide if you can live with what they are suggesting, then go for it whole heartedly if you can.

So let's presume you've given yourself a fighting chance and your face and body you are in the best possible shape; even then it's likely that there are still going to be bits of yourselves that you don't like. Hardly anyone is perfectly proportioned, that's why God (or maybe record companies) created stylists. Believe me there is not a single star that does not enjoy the benefits of a whole range of helpers from make-up artists to hairdressers, stylists and personal trainers.

This is easier with some artists than others. Let's be honest, William Baker, Kylie's best pal and legendary stylist, didn't have the hardest job in the world when he was looking to kit Kylie out for her 'Spinning Around' video. The legendary gold shorts were apparently just knocking about in her wardrobe and when you have an artist with a behind as perfect as Kylie's your job as a stylist is considerably easier. Which does nothing to detract from some of the stunning 'Looks' that William and Kylie created for her 'Show Girl' tour, and where on earth did he find the slinky hoodie for 'Can't Get You Out Of My Head'?

I talk to Chloe Butcher, make-up artist to the stars, later in the chapter, but you won't have access to professionals like them until you've landed a record deal and the most successful artists are also the ones who have a clear idea of their image from the start. So this next section helps you to consider what might be the right 'Look' for you starting with the most dramatic, in-your-face option.

1. 'The Look' that is…Pure Theatre

Writing this book in the summer of 2009, there really was only one contender to represent this Fame Factor and she is Stefani Joanne Angelina Germanotta otherwise known as **Lady Gaga**. A relative newcomer to the charts in her own right, she's been around in her own 'write' (sorry!) for some time, penning songs for Fergie, Pussycat Dolls, Britney, New Kids On The Block and Akon.

Lady Gaga's bonkers fashion style has been variously described as eye-popping, eccentric and outrageous, and as a great publicity stunt to get her noticed; it certainly gets people talking and printing pictures of her. She has been described as a 'fashion maverick with a sense of fun', (the vast majority) or a 'calculated publicity seeker with a touch of the pantomime dame' (a cynical few). In this case the cynics are wrong as Lady Gaga has been following her unique fashion path since high school when she was horribly teased for her inability to follow the fashion herd.

Lady Gaga admits her influences on her website:

"I always loved rock and pop and theater. When I discovered Queen and David Bowie is when it really came together for me and I realized I could do all three…It's not just about the music. It's about the performance, the attitude, the look; it's everything. And, that is where I live as an artist and that is what I want to accomplish."

Lady Gaga reminds me a lot of Elton John, stay with me on this! They are both fine musicians and song writers and she clearly shares his sense of fashion fun since she claims to be trying to *"change the world one sequin at a time"*.

These days Elton is as likely to wear couture suits with a sequin trim but his theatrical costumes have always been pivotal to his performance. This is the man who has appeared on stage as the Statue of Liberty or head to foot in sequins and ostrich feathers; and let's not forget that during the brief time I worked for him (his manager John Reid sacked me because I was too scruffy – it's true!) he also appeared in Central Park in front of half a million people in a Donald Duck costume!

Pure Theatre is all about impact. Here are two more examples that you should check out and then make a list of your personal favourites and see if there's a look amongst them to inspire you.

David Bowie was the original image chameleon and has been a style icon for four decades but he led the way in terms of pure theatre when he created his stage persona of Ziggy Stardust, swiftly followed by Aladdin Sane. Incorporating mime, and sporting full theatrical make-up and skin tight spangled creations, he was a huge influence on the glam rock movement and posed intriguing gender identity questions.

Kylie's Show Girl Tour – it's all in the title, isn't it? – featured dozens of extravagant costume changes including a jewel-encrusted couture corset by John Galliano which took four months to make as each jewel was painstakingly hand sewn. The feathered headdresses, supplied by the famous Lido in Paris, were so big that they needed a truck all of their own to transport them between venues.

This Look does however come with a health warning, 'Pure Theatre' is one of the trickiest and most expensive images to create well, and to really pull it off you need a personality to match, one that's at least as big as your wardrobe truck!

2. Fashion Rocks… the designer 'Look'

In 2003, The Prince's Trust staged 'Fashion Rocks' at the Albert Hall in London and for Channel 4 television; it celebrated the relationship between music and fashion and its premise was very simple. A cast of international music stars would wear an outfit specially designed for them by their chosen designer and as they performed the designer would stage a fashion show around them.

The very first show created some amazing moments as Beyoncé strutted in Armani, Robbie Williams in Versace, and Bjork wore an Alexander McQueen creation and a crystal mask. At later events Bon Jovi, Alicia Keyes, Justin Timberlake, Jay Z, Christina Aguilera and Maria Carey to name but a few paired up with the likes of Chanel, Gucci, Dolce and Gabbana, Prada, Ralph Lauren and Yves Saint Laurent.

From the beginning of pop history, fashion and music have enjoyed a mutually beneficial relationship; one in which the stars get free clothes and the designers get free publicity. In the 70's Vivienne Westwood joined forces with Malcolm McLaren to invent the punk style and have the Sex Pistols propel it to the masses. However, it's often much more than just a business arrangement and designers can be truly inspired by their pop star muses. Jean Paul Gaultier's corset collection for Madonna's Blond Ambition tour was surely a marriage made in heaven resulting in the iconic conical gold bra.

Becoming a top designer's muse does of course require a certain level of success. Ironically just when you can afford a designer or even couture outfits (couture gowns are the ones that are hand stitched for individual clients and can cost tens of thousands of pounds) the designers will often be happy to give you, or at least to lend you, their beautiful clothes. The publicity shots of you wearing their designs are worth more than any number of advertisements.

If you were to be allowed into the hallowed halls of Armani, Chanel or Matthew Williamson before any major red carpet event you would be amazed at the almost constant stream of A-listers popping in for fittings for the gowns (and suits) they will borrow to wear on the big night.

3.Looking like the girl or boy next door…

When we first started working with Kylie, most people were still having trouble pronouncing her surname, it's hard to imagine now but back then she was 'Charlene' from the Neighbours to most people, the feisty young girl in overalls who lived next door to Scott (Jason Donovan). From a purely marketing perspective it was obvious that we should build on Kylie's on screen appeal and tasked our stylist to find her outfits that enhanced her 'girl-next-door' image. At this stage Kylie was too busy with her Neighbours filming schedule to contribute much to her look.

'**The Girl or Boy Next Door Look**' – let your fans think 'that could be me' and love you for it, but beware, this look is just as carefully contrived as the others. The clothes may be more High Street than designer, but you need to convey an image that the fans can admire and aspire to copy without much expense. Westlife,

S Club 7 or Steps may have started out wearing jeans and T shirts but they were perfectly fitting jeans and T shirts and the band's look will have been coordinated right down to the smallest detail. The group's wardrode may look like something put together without much thought, but careful consideration always goes into every decision.

Urban Street Cool and Night Club Sexy are 'Looks' that do what they say on the tin and are loaded with attitude; think Dizzee Rascal and Girls Aloud, so surely they are the total opposite of the innocent girl-next-door? Think again because when you dig a little deeper they actually do the very same thing and provide an accessible image that the fans can aspire to imitate.

Girls Aloud and Sugababes may well be wearing designer labels these days but as Gok Wan is always telling us, with a bit of flair, the fans can recreate this 'Look' from the High Street.

Urban Street Cool with its low slung jeans, tracksuits and backwards baseball caps is an easy look to recreate even if you can't accessorise it with a massive diamond encrusted pendant and designer shades.

Necessity is the mother of all re-invention

This look is all about reinventing a look borrowed from fashion history; believe me top fashion designers and successful artists have been doing this forever so why not take a leaf out of their books and get some inspiration from styles that created a stir in previous decades (and even centuries).

Check out this **Fashion in Music** quiz and see if you don't agree with me that completely new 'Looks' are rare both in music and in fashion. Can you spot the exceptions? Answers on page 61.

1. Disco Inferno

In the late seventies *Saturday Night Fever* revamped the Bee Gees careers with a series of massive hits. Disco was back with a vengeance and at Studio 54, the coolest of cool New York clubs, the dance floor was crammed with bright Lycra leotards and footless tights. Which major star, who clearly avoids Hard Candy, recently revisited this look?

2. Becoming Bee Hives

Back in the early sixties, just before Twiggy burst onto the scene with her urchin cut, a towering blond beehive hairdo was just the thing. It involved hours of backcombing and gallons of hair spray and was famously modeled by the likes of Dusty Springfield and later by the B52's. Which artist went back to black in 2007 with an artfully bedraggled 'updo' that owes much to the original sixties beehive?

3. Military two step

Borrowing from an exaggerated military look that would not have looked out of place on a Russian Cavalryman in the 1800's, and with the help of Vivienne Westwood – again! – Adam Ant cavorted as the Dandy Highwayman in 1981, demanding that we *'Stand and Deliver'*. Who wore brightly coloured military satin on the cover of a famously iconic album released two decades earlier in 1967?

4. Lingering Lingerie

We know that Jean Paul Gaultier took inspiration from his mother's 50's style pink satin corsets when he designed the costumes for Madonna's Blond Ambition tour in 1990. In 2001 which two pop divas stripped off wedding dresses to reveal some slinky bridal lingerie when they joined Madge on stage at the MTV Awards?

5. New Romantics for Old

In the early eighties the New Romantics were looking for an antidote to the aggressively edgy punk stance. Bands like Spandau Ballet and Duran Duran spent the money they saved on gallons of hair gel for the spiky punk Mohicans (another borrowed style!), on frilly flouncy shirts with more than a nod to the dandy's of the Regency period. Can you think of anyone who has revisited this look in the nineties or noughties?

6. Flower Power and Hippie Counter Culture

In 1967 Scott McKenzie sang 'If you're going to San Francisco, be sure to wear some flowers in your hair' to promote the Monterey Pop Festival. Festivals, the hippie look: flowing feminine dresses, headbands and long hair, never really went away but 2009 saw a Broadway revival of an iconic rock musical that celebrates this era – what is it?

7. Barefoot Beauty

Sandy Shaw may possibly have been the coolest artist to ever win The Eurovision Song Contest in 1965 with her Mary Quant hairdo, mini dresses and…bare feet! Which young multi-platinum soul songstress also refuses to wear shoes?

8. Goths and Vampires

The Goth look, modeled by bands like The Cure and Siouxie and The Banshees, followed Punk and included heavy black eye liner worn with a chalk white face and almost exclusively black clothes – I always suspected that it borrowed from some inspiration from classic Hollywood vampires. The question is has anyone adopted this look in the noughties?

9. American Sweethearts

The Andrews Sisters were the forces' sweethearts in the Second World War with hits like 'Boogie Woogie Bugle Boy'. Which singer released a single in 2007 whose musical style and glamorous cover harked back to the era and could have graced the fuselage of any American airman's fighter plane?

10. The Sixties

Possibly the most raided fashion era ever, and the miniskirt truly was an original fashion moment that has never gone away. Which 60's wannabe spiced up her look with a Union Jack mini dress 1997?

My Top Tips

OK, I think you get my point and you know that you have a lot of options to choose from so here are some basic principals to consider:

★ Concentrate on a creating a 'Look' that suits your music and that you can carry off.

★ Consider how your 'Look' is going to work with your Killer Moves. Whether you decide on a leggy Girls Aloud look in towering heels, a hairdo that requires gallons of hairspray, tightly laced corsets or military epaulettes – they all require effort and commitment.

★ Will you be able to cope with a make-up and hair call two hours before everybody else or should you put your hand up right now and decide that a version of the boy or girl next door look is the way for you?

★ Consider how uncomfortable you are prepared to be – Nicola from Girls Aloud says that she is so used to dancing in towering heels on stage that she can no longer comfortably wear flat shoes, even at home.

★ If dramatic heavy make-up is going to be part of your 'Look', you must also take on a proper cleansing routine as it will look less effective over a fresh crop of spots

And always remember the bottom line. This Fame Factor has a job to do and that is to achieve as many as possible of the following for you:

★ Get you noticed
★ Make the fans like/admire/want to be you
★ Add to your PR'ability factor – see also Fame Factor 6 – PR'ability
★ Enhance your music
★ Add to your performance

Help, I'm a singer not a stylist…

I do realise that although some people are blessed with an innate sense of style and others can learn to put a 'Look' together, many of you will find this Fame Factor just a big old nightmare, so here are some ideas to help.

Stuff that you can do…

You may not be able to get the advice of a top stylist but there will be, and closer to home than you might imagine, a whole bunch of talented people that you may be able to talk into helping you – particularly if you are a Pop Star with enough 'Self- Belief' and 'Determination' (see Fame Factors 7 and 4).

Who is the best art or fashion student at your school or college, who has a flair for raiding charity shops and turning retro pieces into unique looks? Talk to them and see if you can get them to team up with you to create your look.

Befriend local designers and artists and convince them to help you to create a 'Look' that might:

★ borrow from history, creating a 'Look' that hasn't recently been revisited
★ take a masculine style that could be given a female twist – or vice versa
★ be something completely new that their creative brains can invent for you

If there a fantastic boutique in your town that would consider sponsoring you in kind by providing some great clothes?

Experiment with make-up yourself and with friends.

Go to a Mac or Bobbi Brown counter within a major department store on a wet Tuesday and get them to give you a free makeover. Don't go on a Saturday when they are busy and trying to make their sales commission. Approach this research professionally, make notes and take a photo with your mobile for reference.

Check out student nights at the best hair salons in your town to try different hair styles .

Some Insider gen from 'Glam Squad' expert -

Chloe Butcher...

Once you have a record deal, your record company will find a make-up artist to work with you. Carol Hayes Management have been booking top make-up artists, hairdressers and stylists since we first started PWL and she put me in touch with make-up artist Chloe Butcher whose credits include Ashley Cole, Cheryl Cole, Donna Air, Edith Bowman, Emma Bunton, Girls Can't Catch, Girls Aloud, Westlife, Gerri Halliwell, Lily Cole, Lisa Snowdon, Melanie Sykes, Mischa Barton and Will Young to name but a few! I asked her some questions for you:

PW. **Typically on a pop video for a new artist who gives you the brief for the look and how much is left up to your discretion?**

CB: From my experience there is quite often a test shoot that happens first in order to put together a team of people; hair, make-up and styling. It allows the band to get used to being in front of the camera and for the glam squad to try out a few different looks to see which direction they should be pushed in.

The director is usually at the forefront of deciding the theme and look of it all. The management and record company would keep a close eye on what is suggested to make sure we don't go completely off the track. The director, make-up, hair and stylist would usually meet before to discuss ideas and look at a mood board and then with all that information in hand the make-up artist would use her own initiative and create the look.

PW. **How much input does the artist have (if any)?**

CB: At the beginning the artist doesn't usually have much input into the look especially if they are young and brand new. As they become more established they will have clearer views on how they want to look and get much more involved.

It is the make-up artist's job to guide them and teach them what works for their face. It is very easy for a teenager to assume everything will look great which is often not the case. There has to be a huge amount of trust between the artist and make-up artist, as this is the person who can make the difference between them looking nice and looking amazing, edgy and glamourous.

PW. **Is it very different working with actors and actresses as opposed to pop stars?**

CB: The main difference is that actors seem to be much less fussed and are slightly more laid back when it comes to their make-up. A few times they haven't even checked themselves in the mirror when I have finished (Mischa Barton & Holly Valance)! My theory is that so often they play roles where they have to look like every day people and very natural, so have the confidence to be happy whether they are dolled up or simply fresh faced. Pop stars always want to look their best.

PW. **Do you ever go on tour with an artist?**

CB: Artists and bands (especially pop) do usually have their glam squad with them so I have toured with Girls Aloud twice and with Kylie when she was promoting her Body Language album, doing make-up for all of her dancers.

Touring with these artists was quite different. I worked with Girls Aloud for three years and became very close to them so being on the tour bus travelling around the UK for seven weeks at a time was brilliant fun despite the hard work. All the girls are very energetic and work incredibly hard on stage, singing and doing big dance routines. The make-up has to be quite full on so it lasts the two hot and sweaty hours.

Working with Kylie was also brilliant and involved a lot of travelling, numerous flights, buses and hotels. Quite often you lose track of which country you are in and what day of the week it is! Kylie is a pop icon and really knows what captivates her audience. She loves to experiment with her look and this translates down to her dancers. The looks were always very dramatic with lots of theatrical make-up, body painting and tons of glitter.

PW. **I'm sure that the boys wear make-up too, but you can't see it – how do you do that?**

CB: It's all about looking immaculate without anyone knowing it has taken two hours to get ready! Trimming and styling the stubble, moisturising, using an anti shine gel followed by a little foundation and concealer. Bronzer is a winner as it gives a healthy glow and can be used to shade the face and chisel the features. Powder, lip balm and a quick tidy up of the eye brows usually does it. Hair is very important.

As with the girls, make-up for boys depends on what the job is for. For example if it was an interview on TV I would use quite a lot of make-up as the lights used are very strong and tend to make people look washed out, pale and shiny.

PW. **What's the longest and most complicated job you've ever done?**

CB: The longest job by far was Girls Aloud's second video for 'No Good Advice'. It started at 6am and went on to 5am the following day. Everything went wrong, outfits ripped, ankles twisted and everyone was absolutely exhausted.

Another long hard shoot was for Westlife's 'Queen Of My Heart' video. There were over 100 dancers and three different looks for each which took an incredibly long time to do. Shooting started very late and went on well into the early hours.

The most complicated job I have been on was one of Kylie's videos. There were over 20 dancers who needed intricate make-up and several looks. I was using gold leaf which is notoriously fiddly, spraying their hands and feet different colours and making them look like they were wearing masks which were actually done directly on the skin with glitter. Despite the pressure being on, as there is always so much to film; I loved it because to be creative like that is what a make-up artist dreams of.

PW. **What's been your favourite job to date and why?**

CB: I love any job that allows me to show off my creative flair. I have drawn and painted for most of my life and that is what I studied at college. To me, make-up was a natural progression and I really enjoy making people look beautiful, changing appearances, creating new styles and being artistic.

My favourite job to date was Girls Aloud's first tour, 'What Will The Neighbours Say'. It was all so new and fresh and everybody was enthusiastic and full of energy. The looks were great, strong and sexy and the vibe was brilliant. However, what made this so memorable for me was this is where I met my husband, guitarist Peter Honoré. He was in the band and we fell in love the moment we met on the tour bus!

PW. **Which artist's 'Look' (current or classic look from the past) do you most admire?**

CB: Oh my goodness, this is such a hard one and very difficult to answer. I admire so many artists and so many looks. I love Gwen Stefani; she is daring but always looks amazing and has a very keen eye for style. Madonna and Pink are both fantasticas they aren't afraid to be different and change their lo oks frequently.

I love how Christina Aguilera and all the other girls looked in the Moulin Rouge video. Kylie looked striking and iconic in 'Can't Get You Out Of My Head' and Girls Aloud looked dark and edgy in 'Sexy No No No'."

Answers to the Fashion in Music quiz

1. Madonna
2. Amy Winehouse
3. The Beatles on the cover of Sergeant Pepper's Lonely Hearts Club Band
4. Britney Spears and Christina Aguilera
5. It's a trick question to get you thinking and researching – I couldn't think of anyone, can you? Maybe it's time for a re-invention?
6. Hair
7. Joss Stone
8. I don't think so but since Edward and Bella's vampire romance in Twilight is proving to have huge book and box office appeal, perhaps it's time for some modern day Goths to re-emerge from their darkened rooms
9. Christina Aguilera – Candy Man
10. Spice Girl Geri Halliwell

FAME FACTOR 4

DETERMINATION

To be honest I think that this Fame Factor – Determination – is either in your DNA or it's not, but sometimes it might just need activating and hopefully this chapter will get you thinking and examining your own level of commitment.

How often have you known the mildest, seemingly un-ambitious people to come out fighting when it's for something they really believe in? In this case the thing you have to believe in is yourself. 'Determination' and 'Self-Belief' are inextricably linked but this Fame Factor is the one about dogged persistence in the face of adversity.

Let me jump straight in with the icon who best embodies this for me and instead of a pop star I'm going to talk about my old friend, Simon Cowell, who I first met when he was almost stalking me at the PWL studios.

At the time Stock Aitken Waterman were the hottest producers on the block and Simon was a small time label manager looking for a hit record. He was desperate for us to work with one of his acts and every time I turned around he was there with another act, or a song, or an idea he thought could be a hit.

Simon is the first to admit that in those days he really hadn't quite figured out what made a hit record, but he said in a Daily Mail interview recently that he learnt all he knows about judging pop acts from me, which is very flattering.

> *"If I'm ever cruel"* Simon says, *"it's because show business is cruel but I've learned much over the years from Pete Waterman – real tough love. He once said to me 'You don't know what you're talking about'. You're bloody useless. Come back when you've got a hit. I took it as a challenge. I don't like bull**** I don't like hype."*
>
> Daily Mail 23.5.09

The fact is that I turned Simon and his suggestions away dozens of times but in the end he turned up with Sinitta with whom we had five top 20 hits. Simon was on his way to becoming a very successful A&R and label manager, and we went on to have hits with him with Five and Westlife.

Simon appears to have mellowed quite a bit recently in his judging role on 'Britain's Got Talent' but he is still capable of whipping out one of the cruel put downs or merciless criticisms that made him famous at the beginning of his TV career. People also tend to forget that in the early days, some of the braver contestants were keen to remind him of moments in his career that might have made him rich but had hardly bought him musical credibility.

This is the man who gave us The World Wrestling Federation, the Mighty Morphin' Power Rangers and Robson and Jerome; I've still not forgiven him for the number of times I have subsequently had to sit through terrible audition performances of 'Unchained Melody'. And what on earth was 'Mr Nasty' doing with Tinky Winky, Laa Laa and their cuddly Teletubby friends? The answer was simple, making money and being very successful.

Amidst these lucrative but less credible successes, Simon also masterminded a string of hits and massive success for Five, Il Divo and Westlife, but he has always been completely undaunted by negative comments and his rise from a small time label manager to one of the richest and most famous men in entertainment, both sides of the Atlantic, is truly remarkable. Last time I went to America I was absolutely gobsmacked to see Simon's face smiling down at me from a huge billboard. It was like being back in the 80's, he was still stalking me!

Simon's greatest talent is his ability to spot a good idea and to capitalise on it and not to let anything get in the way of his determination to make it work. By spotting and capitalising on the seemingly insatiable appetite for TV talent shows, and by creating the 'X Factor' and 'Britain's Got Talent' franchises, he has become one of the most powerful men in TV.

'Determination' is all about picking yourself up from the last knock back and hurling yourself back with as much enthusiasm and attack at the next challenge that presents itself.

Determination – how do you measure up…?

So, if you're wondering whether you have the required determination or if you're convinced that you have, try this little quiz and measure yourself against the stars who score 10 out of 10 for determination. You get bonus points for correctly identifying the artists upon whom the stories are based – they are revealed at the end of the quiz.

1. **You have done extremely well to become the runner up in a TV music talent show but now your five minutes of fame is beginning to wane and you have the opportunity to take part in another TV challenge show. The skills required are a good way outside of your comfort zone; do you:**
a) Turn it down, you think your chances of winning are slim and you don't want to be known as the runner up in everything you do?
b) Take it on; it's TV exposure even if you are knocked out early on in the series?
c) Take on the challenge, give it 150% and win?

2. **You are half way through a gruelling challenge for Comic Relief, you have a minor but excruciating injury and the paparazzi trailing you are hinting that there is a scandal brewing at home; do you:**
a) Retire gracefully but genuinely injured – you've done your best but the challenge is much harder than you had imagined and you need to get home?
b) Soldier on for another day then retire hurt; you'll gain brownie points for the extra effort when you are clearly in pain, but completing the challenge is frankly just asking too much?
c) Soldier on, complete the challenge and raise thousands for charity?

3. **You have launched your own small record label, which has used up all your financial resources and the phone hasn't rung for almost a week; do you:**
a) Give the whole business up and go back to being paid to work for other record labels, the pop industry is like shifting sand and you can be hot one week and stone cold the next?

b) Set yourself a deadline, if business hasn't picked up within the next six weeks, you'll get ready to call it a day. You have a good string of hits behind you as a record producer but that doesn't mean there is any guarantee of future success?

c) Get another bank loan to pay the bills and call all your contacts again to generate some work?

4. Your last record was a flop and your recently ex-husband has taken up with the next hot new pop star on the block. Your manager says you've been offered a chance to take part in a dance show that is the polar opposite of your cool image; do you:

a) Turn it down – you are a credible artist not a light entertainment puppet?

b) Agree to take part, you are desperate and there's a fee involved?

c) Take part, embrace the experience, have the time of your life and win?

5. Your band has reached the semi final of a live talent show 50 miles from your home town. The prize is a slot on a TV show but you've been beaten on the clappometer by the local band who had more supporters in the theatre; do you:

a) Go back to playing local clubs and earning pin money?

b) Put in some more rehearsals – there's always next year?

c) Get a new drummer and check out the manager of the local record shop who has offered to manage you?

6. It's the night before a major TV appearance, it's also your boyfriend's/girlfriend's birthday. He/she is demanding that you go out and party, your manager is insisting on an early night, you have a 6.30am call. Do you:

a) Sneak out of the hotel and back without anyone realising; you can cope with very little sleep and you don't want to risk losing your boyfriend/girlfriend?

b) Convince your boyfriend/girlfriend to bring the champagne to your hotel room and sneak him into the hotel?

c) Get the early night: if your boyfriend/girlfriend loves you they will just have to understand?

7. You've just walked out of an X Factor audition after Simon Cowell told you had a boring voice. Do you:

a) Take him at his word and dine out on the experience for the next 6 months?

b) Cry but wake up the next day and consider whether he might have a point and is there anything you can do to find a more identifiable voice?

c) Ignore him; Simon Cowell can have an off day like anyone else?

Mostly A's...

You give up at the first hurdle, and I'm sorry but I don't think you have the mental strength to survive in a business that is full of knock backs.

Mostly B's...

You do move forward in the face of a challenge but only until the next one checks your progress. To really make it you need to give everything 150% not 90%.

Mostly C's...

You're right up there with Simon Cowell in seeing each set back as a new challenge to be overcome and with that attitude that's exactly what you have a good chance of doing.

'How determined Are You' Quiz...
The names and the faces behind the stories

1. Ray Quinn
About a year ago I spotted a poster telling me that 'Ray Quinn is Danny' advertising a West End run of 'Grease' the musical. I'm sure I wasn't alone in thinking, who's Ray Quinn? I was reminded that he was one of the runners up in the X Factor.

He was offered a place in Torville and Dean's ITV show 'Dancing On Ice' which was a bit of a gamble and not necessarily the most relevant move you might think for a singer, not to mention the real risk of injury for an artist who needed to dance as well as sing.

However, what the show actually did was to showcase Ray's determination and passion and his fantastic dancing ability; and I have it on very good authority from the show's producers that he was an absolute delight to work with.

Ray put his heart and soul into the challenge, was an inspiration to watch and won the series. The result: acres of news coverage and a whole new legion of fans who would not be questioning who Ray Quinn was the next time he opened in the West End – which is where, as I write, he is currently starring once again as Danny in Grease.

2. Cheryl Cole
In early 2009, Cheryl Cole climbed Kilimanjaro with a bunch of celebrities including band mate Kimberley for the Comic Relief charity. She made it to the top despite carrying a toe injury that she had sustained during preparations for the climb and despite the fact that before reaching the top she was told that her husband, the footballer Ashley Cole, had been arrested for being drunk and disorderly outside a nightclub and was splashed across all the tabloid papers.

3. Pete Waterman

So there we were in our new office, me and my new business partner David Croker, who I had worked with at Rocket Records. I had ploughed all my money into the business and the phones were so silent that on the third day I got David to go down the road to a pay phone and call the office number just to make sure we hadn't been cut off.

The work finally started to pick up and when I started building my first studio at the Vineyard (which would eventually have three state-of-the-art studios) I had ploughed everything into building it and had to sleep at the studio as I had nowhere else to live. The receptionist got used to seeing me emerge from the basement into reception first thing in the morning with my towel and toothbrush.

4. Alesha Dixon

When Alesha Dixon agreed to take part in 'Strictly Come Dancing' she was at a real low point in her life and her career. After early success as a member or Mis-Teeq and some success with her solo career, she was without a record deal and had recently spit up with her husband MC Harvey from So Solid Crew, having discovered that he was having an affair with Javine Hylton.

Alesha took to the ballroom dance floor with such passion and enthusiasm that she not only won the series but completely revitalised her career and won legions of new fans.

5. Johnny and The Moondogs… who!?

In 1959, a group called 'Johnny and The Moondogs' made the final rounds of a TV star search; the prize was an appearance on Carroll Levi's TV show. The final heat was in Manchester at the Hippodrome Theatre and they lost on the results of the clappometer. Having got that far and failed, they could have given up at that point but three of the band members: John Lennon, Paul McCartney and George Harrison were determined enough to carry on!

6. Several artists I won't name

You know the ones who opted for option a) or b) – they may get away with it once or twice but it's a rocky road and not one you should follow

7. Could it be you?

If it is, this is where you have to figure out whether b) or c) was the best answer and when to temper determination with a realistic assessment of your abilities – see also Fame Factor 7 – Self-Belief.

And Finally…

Having looked at some of the determination displayed by the successful people in this chapter, here are some final thoughts you to take away:

★ Once you have committed to something, don't give up however difficult it becomes (Cheryl on Mount Kilimanjaro).

★ Keep an open mind about the opportunities that present themselves (Alesha).

★ Once you have committed to something give it 150% (Ray and Alesha).

★ If an A&R person doesn't like your material but you still really believe in it, find another A&R person who does.

★ If a door is slammed in your face (like I did to Simon Cowell) and you know they have a point, go away, get better at what you do and go back and knock on the door again.

STAMINA

When you first picked this book up and read my list of required Fame Factors, I wouldn't mind betting that many of you questioned why you needed 'Stamina' to be a pop star. OK, you need to be relatively fit to perform a live show for two hours every night, but how exhausting can it be to perform one song on a TV show?

If you've been paying attention you may be less sceptical by now but in case you still don't quite get it, let's take a look at the sheer physical 'Stamina' you need to be a successful pop star. (For mental stamina, which is equally if not even more important, rewind to Fame Factor 4 – 'Determination' or fast forward to Fame Factor 7 – 'Self-Belief').

I talked about the importance of taking a professional approach to your body in Fame Factor 3 – The Look. Getting into shape and eating healthily is a pre-requisite for looking fantastic but it's also vital to maintain the 'Stamina' a modern pop star needs. We're going to look at some typical schedules and you can start working out how long the days are and how much sleep you're going to get, bearing in mind that pop stars are expected to sparkle constantly!

In your first year you are going to be meeting hundreds of new people who are going to talk or write about you via every possible media outlet and you need to always remember:

You will have just one opportunity to make a great impression on them! What they say will be vital to how the public perceive you.

The only way people are going to find out about you is through media coverage. Most people will make up their mind about you the first time they see, hear or read about you.

So your task is simple – you must approach each interview and performance as if it is your only chance to make it and you therefore need to be charming, looking your best and fully engaged, even if you are feeling totally exhausted. Are you beginning to get the picture? Then read on.

Kylie – early days...

As we all know Kylie Minogue is small but perfectly formed, and believe it or not she doesn't have huge natural energy reserves within that tiny frame; which makes her enduring 'Stamina' all the more remarkable. To be honest I could just as easily have chosen her as my shining example of 'Determination' (or most of the other Fame Factors) but I chose 'Stamina' because I think that it has been her biggest challenge.

At the start of her singing career Kylie was also filming a busy and demanding schedule in Neighbours as Charlene Mitchell. For those of you who don't remember, she and Scott Robinson (Jason Donovan) were taking faltering steps forward in their rocky relationship. Over 19 million viewers watched when they finally made it down the aisle. ('Especially For You', her duet with Jason went to Number 1 in the charts later that year – but that's another story see Fame Factor 9 – Public Appeal).

Kylie's filming commitments meant that we only had her for short periods of time which we had to negotiate with Channel 10, the TV Company that produced Neighbours in Melbourne. When you look at her schedule below, which is a recreation of the week that we released 'The Locomotion', Kylie's second UK hit, remember that she also had to add a twenty-three hour flight and a nine hour time difference to the equation. Most fledgling pop stars won't have this additional pressure but their promotion schedules are likely to look very similar.

Today the names and the programmes will of course have changed and when we were promoting 'The Locomotion' in the summer of 1988, the World Wide Web was hardly more than a gleam in the eyes of some geeky computer experts in Silicon Valley. However, you can expect to work at this kind of pace for at least the first couple of years if you want to be a success, and have a great record company behind you. (See Fame Factor 8 – Supporting Cast).

Promo Schedule August 1988
– Kylie Minogue – 'The Locomotion'

Monday
06.50   Overnight flight from Melbourne arrives at London Heathrow
07.30   Clear customs – meet driver (and possible paparazzi) at arrivals
        - drive to hotel
08.30   Check in at hotel – shower – breakfast
09.30   Pick up from hotel – drive to Pineapple Dance studios
10.15   Meet choreographer and dancers – work on routine for
        'Locomotion'
13.00   Lunch – Sharp End will go through the week's schedule
        with you
14.00   Resume rehearsals
17.00   Car to hotel
19.00   Dinner at hotel

Tuesday
08.30   Meet stylist at hotel for initial fittings
09.30   Car to Pineapple
10.15   Choreography rehearsals with dancers
13.00   Lunch
14.00   Interview at studio with Smash Hits
14.30   Interview at studio – Radio Times
15.00   Complete choreography with dancers
17.00   Meet Stylist at studio – confirm TV outfits – final fittings
18.00   Car to Radio 1
18.30   Live on Air interview Radio 1
19.15   Car to hotel
20.00   Dinner with PWL MD and staff – a welcome to London

Wednesday
08.00   Hair and make-up at hotel
09.15   Car to BBC TV Centre
10.00   Call time for first camera rehearsal Top of the Pops
10.45   Photo session at TV Centre for Radio Times
11.45   Call time for second camera rehearsal Top of the Pops
12.15   Lunch
13.15   TV Interview for BBC Breakfast – pre-record at TV Centre

13.45	Interview – Just 17 Magazine
14.15	Interview – Daily Mirror
14.45	Into costume for dress rehearsal
15.15	Call time for Top of the Pops dress run
16.00	Phone interviews with local radio stations
	16.05 - Piccadilly Radio (Manchester)
	16.25 - BRMB (Birmingham)
	16.45 - Radio Clyde (Glasgow)
17.05	Retouch make-up, hair
18.30	Call time for Top of the Pops – record 'as live'
20.30	Clear
21.00	Dinner

Thursday

| 10.00 | Car to PWL |
| 11.00 | Recording for album |

During the day we will fit in 3 short local radio interviews. No photos today or face to face interviews but there will be fans outside the studio

| 17.00 | Car to hotel for stylist meeting for photo session and 'Going Live' |

Friday

08.00	Hair at hotel
09.00	Car to photographer's studio
09.45	Make-up
11.00	Photo session – 5 looks for next single, album and promo shots
	Lunch will be provided at the studio
19.00	Drive to Capital Radio
19.45	Neil Fox interview – LIVE to air
20.30	Meet and greet – Capital Radio competition winners
21.15	Clear – car to hotel

Saturday

05.30	Hair and make-up at hotel
07.00	Car to BBC TV Centre
08.00	Call time for 'Going Live' Camera Rehearsal performance
08.30	Meet Philip Schofield – talk through interview
	Meet Producer – walk through participation in 'Trevor & Simon' sketch (script attached)

09.30	Wardrobe plus complete hair and make-up
10.15	Interview with Philip Schofield – LIVE to Air
11.00	Trevor and Simon Sketch - LIVE to Air
11.30	Final camera rehearsal during VT then straight to Performance 'Locomotion' LIVE to Air
12.00	Meet and Greet Competition Winners
12.30	Clear – car to restaurant Afternoon and evening free

Sunday

06.00	Pick up from hotel
07.00	Check in at Heathrow – Terminal 3
09.00	Flight departs for Melbourne

THANKS A MILLION KYLIE AND LOOK FORWARD TO SEEING YOU NEXT TIME!

Kylie scores 9 out of 10 for Stamina...

Despite the demands put on her Kylie was always a delight to work with and a complete professional. Her records soon started to chart in Europe (she would go on to have hits all over the world), so a flight to a different country every few days and a whole new set of international TV's and interviews had to be built into the schedule. Shane Lynch is on record as saying that when Boyzone reached this stage in their career it was this kind of unrelenting schedule that almost sent him completely off the rails.

Sometime in 1989 Kylie got her first ever German TV booking, a live broadcast and their equivalent of Top of the Pops with many millions of viewers. Kylie is mentally resilient and built up her physical defences by eating healthily but, spending so much time on a plane, she was prone to picking up colds and bugs.

She arrived at the TV station with a horrible fluey cold, aching all over and exhausted, having been unable to sleep on the flight from Melbourne just two days earlier. Since she was blowing her nose every few minutes, she decided there was no point doing her make-up until the last minute so she dragged herself into the studio for the first camera run through looking like death warmed up.

She was clearly just going through the motions of her performance, checking camera angles, being perfectly polite to the director but hardly the sparkling and charismatic star we had convinced the producer to book onto this important show. The rehearsal completed, Kylie went back to her dressing room, checked her call time for the actual show, then asked to be brought some hot honey and lemon for her throat an hour before her call; she asked not to be woken up until then.

Sally Atkins, who managed all of Kylie's promotional schedules for PWL, knew that an hour was just enough time to get her hair and make-up done and onto set. With almost any other artist she would have built in an additional half an hour for safety but she was confident that if Kylie said she could pull it together in an hour, she would. The worried TV producer took more convincing; it was a live broadcast after all.

Kylie was on set ten minutes before her call time. The make-up hid her pallor but she still looked pretty dreadful and the producer was hovering, not at all convinced by Sally's reassurances. All too quickly for him, the host of the show was suddenly introducing Kylie in German, the red light on her close up camera went on and she transformed as if by magic!

Her eyes sparkled; she smiled into the camera, executed the dance routine flawlessly and became the star that she is for the full three and a half minutes required. After which, once she was sure the cameras were all turned elsewhere, she slumped onto the nearest riser asking how quickly the car could get them back to the hotel as she needed as much sleep as possible to get through the next day's schedule.

On another memorable occasion she and Jason were at the hotel the evening before they were due to appear on Breakfast TV. It was just before Christmas and they were promoting 'Especially For You' in an attempt to gain the Christmas number one. It had been a particularly mad week as the paparazzi had chased them all over London, desperate to get a picture of the two of them together to prove the rumours of the off-screen romance that Kylie and Jason still wanted to keep under wraps.

Their call time was for 6.30am the following day but around 7pm the night before Jason called to say that Kylie was being violently sick. She had no intention of cancelling their appearance; she was just asking if a doctor could give her something to get her through the show.

The doctor was dispatched but an hour later we got a call from our promotion company to say that their appearance was cancelled. Tragically it was also the night of the Lockerbie plane bombing, when a Boeing 747 crashed into a small Scottish town killing everyone on board and eleven people on the ground. Understandably all of the following morning's coverage was to be concentrated on the disaster. The pair went directly to the airport with even less enthusiasm for a twenty-three hour flight than usual.

Comeback Kylie

When Kylie announced that she had breast cancer in 2005 and was forced to cancel the rest of her 'Show Girl Greatest Hits' tour, she received hundreds of thousands of letters willing her back to full health. The fans who had bought tickets were obviously hoping they would get to see her perform again but not a single one of them would have been surprised if she had decided to completely scale down her performance. Instead Kylie came back with her triumphant 'Show Girl the Homecoming' tour, and an only slightly reworked version of her most lavish production to date with its amazing choreography and multiple costume changes.

Kylie is the consummate professional and I have to award her a star for her 'Stamina' Fame Factor but if I had to really break it down I would rate it as a challenged, but impressive, 9.

Touring and no let up on the pressure...

Ask any artist what their ideal schedule would be on a touring show day and most will vote for a late start with nothing to worry about other than their performance that night. If you are Madonna it may include a session with her personal trainer or some intense yoga to get 'into the zone', however most artists will usually arrive at the venue several hours before their onstage time to give them time to prepare.

The legendary riders demanded by some artists actually reflect the amount of time they spend backstage in their dressing room area which could be up to 20 hours in a week of shows at one venue.

We've all read the stories about Mariah Carey's demands for puppies and kittens but promoters are used to meeting all kinds of requests; anything from Jools Holland who used to ask for a set of local postcards and stamps to Elton's stipulation that he must have satellite TV reception; as a director of Watford Football Club he needs to catch all the televised football coverage before heading to the stage.

Every manager I have ever known has fought to preserve a show day purely focused on performance, but in the commercial world they also want their artists to sell as many records as possible and the promoter and sponsor will be applying pressure to create as much 'noise' as possible around the tour.

Girls Aloud will perform to up to a million people on a three month sell out arena tour but they may still have to talk to Chris Moyles at Radio One at some ungodly hour on the first day of the London leg of the tour, even if they have come off stage in Manchester the night before and driven overnight to London. They might even have to schedule a major TV appearance in the middle of a tour simply because a performance on a prime time Saturday Night programme like 'Strictly Come Dancing' could get them nine million viewers in a single hit.

The live countdown begins…

So if the flow of their day as they gear up for the night's performance is frequently interrupted with interviews and TV appearances, surely once they get to the venue all our pop stars will have to think about is the show – well almost.

Every artist has their particular routine to prepare each night for a demanding two hour show. Some need to hang out with the band, hyping up the excitement levels, some need quiet time on their own, and more than a few seem to need to create a drama of some kind to get their adrenalin going – no names no pack drill! However, before they get to the moment when they explode onto the stage, there is still plenty to be done.

Sound check

The first thing most artists will do on arrival at the venue is the sound check. This means getting on stage with all of the musicians and backing singers, checking the microphone levels and checking their monitor mix. Every venue is different, even those that appear to be very similar and the acoustics can vary enormously even from night to night in the same venue depending on the number and formation of tickets sold.

These days most, if not all, singers use 'in ear' monitors which look like small hearing aids and feed a balanced mix of all the instruments, your vocals and the rest of the bands' vocals into your earpiece. It's a bit like listening to your mp3 player but the mix is designed so that you can hear yourself which is crucial for staying in tune.

The Meet and Greet

So, sound check completed, surely now you can just concentrate on your pre-show rituals: checking your costume changes, relaxing into hair and make-up, doing vocal warm ups. Alas no, most days you will still have to negotiate the 'Meet and Greet'.

A 'Meet and Greet' is a 10, 20 or 30 minute window where the star or stars are wheeled in to meet, sign autographs and be nice to a room full of people who have, for whatever reason, secured a place at this exclusive audience. It can take place at a radio or TV station but most frequently it will be at the venue an hour or so before the show.

Typically there will be about 40 people in the room, mostly fans and competition winners. They will almost always include some disabled or very poorly children for whom a charity has secured an audience, and often some VIP guests – a privilege secured as part of the sponsorship package. Frankly if I were a pop star I would soon begin to dread walking into a room and being nice to a bunch of strangers when all you want to do is to get ready for your show (and meeting poorly children is always upsetting).

The truth is, however, that the best and most successful pop stars take these 'Meet and Greets' in their stride and send a bunch of fans away with not just an autograph and a goody bag, but precious memories of a once in a lifetime experience.

And Finally...

And finally it's time to get on with the job in hand and give an incredible performance for all those screaming fans who have spent their hard earned cash on coming to see you. They deserve the best show you can possibly do – every single night. That'll be just two hours of singing, dancing and sweating under the heat of the spotlights – after what you've been through it will be a piece of cake.

Even perfect pop stars with natural stamina have to work hard to maintain the levels required. See how you measure up in the quiz below.

Measuring your Stamina Fame Factor...

1. Robbie Williams is a keen footballer which is handy since his arena stage can be about half the size of a football pitch. How much physical exercise do you do in a week?

a) None

b) Dancing for a couple of hours every week when I go out with my mates

c) Dancing when I go out plus at least 2 hours at the either the gym, aerobics classes or playing a sport

2. You've had a big night out after an exhausting week and your manager has just told you that you have an extra interview tomorrow at Radio 1 on the breakfast show and the car will be picking you up at the hotel at 7.30am. Do you:

a) Roll out of bed the third time your manager calls you from reception, it's not fair to spring last minute schedule changes on you?

b) Get to reception on time but without bothering to wash your hair or worrying too much about what you're wearing? It's only radio after all!

c) Get a wake-up call for an hour and half before you're due to leave so you can make sure you are looking your best. Radio 1 is hugely important and there are bound to be fans and photographers outside the studio?

3. How do you feel about flying and travelling to new countries?

a) I'm terrified of flying and find foreign travel quite stressful

b) I'm fine flying if I've had a few drinks before I get on board and I do get a bit stressed about packing but I enjoy it once I get there

c) Flying is exciting because it's taking you to new countries and experiences

4. How many illegal 'sickies' have you thrown in the last year?

a) Probably about 3 weeks' worth altogether, my job/college course is dead boring

b) The usual I guess – about 3 or 4

c) None. I genuinely had a dreadful cold and took a few days off

5. Get a DVD of your favourite artist's latest live tour and dance along with them. How far through the show do you get?

a) You're puffing after the first three numbers

b) You managed the first half but then had to give up and how do they manage the costume changes so quickly?

c) All the way through to the encore

6. It's the end of a very long day of interviews and the fans are waiting outside the radio station in the rain – some of them have been there for hours, do you:

a) Make a sneaky exit out of the back door? If you stop and sign autographs you're going to be even later for dinner?

b) Go out of the front door, say hello to the fans but tell them nicely that you're really sorry you don't have time to do autographs today?

c) Get a big umbrella and sign for the fans? There are only 30 or so it will only take about half an hour

7. How long do you see you career lasting?

a) I'll be happy if I can have one hit

b) I know it's difficult but Westlife have been together and having hits for ten years; if I work hard that could be me

c) If I'm lucky enough to make it I can't imagine ever wanting to stop – Madonna is an amazing role model

8. You are on your tenth interview of the day and the journalist keeps getting your name wrong, do you:

a) Storm out of the interview, if he can't be bothered to do his research you can't be bothered to answer his questions?

b) Complete the interview as quickly as possible then rant at your manager for not vetting the interviewers more carefully?

c) Put him right and make a joke of it, then finish the interview?

Mostly A's...

I seriously think you should reconsider your choice of career, and to maybe seriously consider your level of commitment to life in general and your willingness to embrace new experiences.

Mostly B's...

Could definitely do better, you might just about get through a pop star itinerary but you probably wouldn't get booked onto the next one as you don't have the 150% commitment required.

Mostly C's...

You have the commitment, attitude and energy to make a successful pop star. You realise how important it is to always be nice to your fans and that you only have one chance to make a great first impression.

Stuff you can do…

★ Get fit and eat a healthy diet. Is this starting to sound familiar? Well don't just take it from me – Girls Aloud's 'Dreams That Glitter' autobiography has lots of interesting stuff on the rigours of being a touring pop star and coping physically with the demands.

★ We talked about the importance of having a distinctive voice in Fame Factor 2, but remember that your voice is also a muscle and needs warming up and constant exercise to maintain it, especially for the rigours of a tour. Get into the habit of doing this every day.

★ Consider the advantages of sharing the load by becoming a band member rather than a solo artist (check out Fame Factor 8 – Supporting Cast)

★ Consider whether you can seriously cope with looking great every single day, constantly meeting and being nice to new people and being in a different hotel room every single night

★ If you are genuinely scared of flying, focus on the fact that over 67 million passengers a year safely take off and land at Heathrow Airport in London, multiply that by the number of airports around the world and consider just how rarely anything goes wrong – and if that fails consider a professional hypnotherapy course because flying is going to be a big and important part of your success

★ Make sure your manager is experienced enough to understand the balance between what is ideal for your career and what is possible (see also Fame Factor 8 – Supporting Cast)

PR'ABILITY

What is 'PR'ability' and why do I need it?

OK, I'm going to contradict myself immediately here and say that although 'PR'ability' is a Fame Factor 'must-have', some of the songs I talked about in chapter one are so brilliant that they will break through without any perceptible media coverage. However, let me also say that these are as rare as hen's teeth!

Since the birth of pop music in the fifties, pop stars have been launching or promoting their careers with headline-grabbing publicity stunts. Today the outlets for media exposure may have changed enormously, but in these days of instant media access and a miniscule attention span it's even more important to stand out from the crowd. If you're wondering why it's so important, just think about it this way.

Every week a clutch of new artists arrive on the scene, bright-eyed and bushy-tailed and full of confidence. Every year at least 90% of them disappear without a trace and without you ever hearing of them. The reason is that there is only a finite amount of radio and TV airtime, there are simply far more records released than there are hours in the day available to play them. These shiny new artists are not only competing with each other for airtime but with the whole spectrum of established artists. Added to which the general public only has a limited amount of cash to spend on music or DVD's.

One of my first jobs in the music business was promoting records for various record labels and when you're trying to get the attention of a DJ or their producer, you just can't walk in every week and tell them that every single record you are asking them to play is 'fantastic' (even if you think it is!). You need something else to catch their attention and make them keen to hear more about the artist. You need a story.

However even once you've got your record being played on the radio or in the clubs, the same principle applies to winning over the public. I've already talked about three crucial Fame Factors that you need the public to know and love about you: The Songs, The Voice and The Look; they have to be distinctive so that people immediately make the connection to you as an artist. If you've also managed to do something that's got you a million hits on YouTube or onto the front page of daily newspaper, the chances are they're going to at pay just a little bit more attention.

The Fame Factor I'm calling 'PR'ability' is all about the skills you need to achieve this, the pitfalls you should be aware of and some of the most impressive, effective or downright misguided examples of 'PR'ability' from the annals of pop history.

Which brings me neatly to the pop icon I have chosen to best represent 'PR'ability'. Ladies and gentlemen I give you ... the Spice Girls and 'Girl Power'!

Creating a Media 'Spice World'

My number one tip when you are thinking about your own 'PR'ability' Fame Factor is to take a leaf out of the Spice Girls' book and to remember the simple fact that the most effective PR story is the one that is 100% believable.

It's almost impossible to think of the Spice Girls crashing onto the pop scene without picturing them thrusting their arms into the air and shouting 'Girl Power!' The Spice Girls and Girl Power dominated the media for most of 1996. We watched them hugging Nelson Mandela, hob-nobbing at number 10 with Tony Blair and inappropriately kissing HRH Prince Charles at his Prince's Trust 21st anniversary concert (when they told him he was very sexy and that they could spice up his life) and it's unlikely that any of these things would have happened without their empowering battle cry.

Girl Power was a brilliant catchphrase, I'm not even sure that it was a brilliant PR plan, it could have been something said in an interview that the media picked up on. However, once the girls and their record company saw the media reaction to it they were certainly savvy enough to milk it for all it was worth and ran a full page add in Smash Hits magazine in July 1996 that read:

"Wanted – anyone with a sense of freedom and adventure. Hold tight, get ready, Girl Power is comin' at you".

That sounds a bit cynical on my part, I don't mean it to be because the girls genuinely believed in Girl Power, and because they believed in it, it became true. They even got away with claims like Geri's that "Maggie (Thatcher) was the first Spice Girl!"

`At a time when girls were suddenly outshining the boys at school, and just before the worst excesses of 'ladette' culture had fully established itself, here were five girls who walked straight into the hearts of millions of pre-teenage girls for the simple reason that their fans could totally identify with them.

When Peter Loraine, then editor of *Top of the Pops* magazine gave each Spice Girl a name that encapsulated their image and personalities, he handed them a moment of PR and marketing genius. Who doesn't secretly still think of them as Baby, Sporty, Posh, Ginger and Scary? Every young girl could identify with one of the Spice Girls and the device instantly gave the media five different angles to run with.

I said at the beginning that the stories that work best are the genuine ones and once again the Spice Girls hit that right on the button. They had Girl Power, they had instantly memorable names and identities and 'Wannabe', their first and massive hit, was all about a friendship that never ends!

Once again the PR story was spot on. Even though we all followed what came much later – the acrimonious splits, resignations by fax and subsequent reunions; at the start of their career we totally believed that the girls were going to be friends for life.

It's no secret that the Spice Girls were a manufactured band by which I mean that they were auditioned and put together by their first manager Chris Herbert, but by the time they had a hit record they had genuinely become five great friends having a whale of a time.

Historic Headlines

The Spice Girls were of course only following in a long tradition. I don't think Colonel Tom Parker ever told Elvis to deliberately outrage the American matrons with his gyrating hips but it caused a media storm at the time, not to mention near riots when he performed and it definitely helped put the boy from Memphis well and truly on the map.

Record company press officers and canny managers have always understood the power of a controversial headline and with every new artist they sign they are always looking for something to get their artist noticed. It might be a stunt, a connection to an existing star is always helpful, or it might simply entail bringing the media's attention to a genuine phenomenon.

Take a look at the headlines below; they illustrate what I'm talking about. You can decide for yourself how well you think they worked and whether you agree with the saying that there is no such thing as bad, or even too much publicity. The stories below include a couple that almost derailed the artist's career.

Do something controversial

1966: When interviewed by a reporter for London's Evening Standard, John Lennon claims that The Beatles 'were bigger than Jesus'.

1977 EMI drop the Sex Pistols after packers at the factory refuse to handle the punk band's single 'Anarchy In the UK'; they were disgusted by the band's spitting and swearing.

1983 Radio 1 bans Frankie Goes To Hollywood's sexually explicit first single 'Relax', despite it having already reached number 6 in the chart.

1989 Madonna causes outrage with the Catholic Church when the 'Like A Virgin' video, which features burning crosses and statues weeping blood, is released.

Do something first

1964   The Supremes become the first ever all girl group to top the US Record charts with their single 'Baby Love'.

1987   At just 16, Tiffany is the youngest act after Michael Jackson to reach the number one slot with her single 'I Think We're Alone Now'.

Do something topical

1969   David Bowie celebrates the moon landing with the release of the new 'Space Oddity' single.

1977   New, young multi-racial band from Birmingham take their name from the UB40 social security form.

1977   The Jam lead Mod revival with their 'In The City' single.

Do something to create some chaos

1995   The Spice Girls shock race goers at Kempton Park by clambering over Desert Orchid.

1997   Security alert as HRH Prince Charles gets a taste of Girl Power when two of the Spice Girls breach royal protocol and kiss the Prince.

2001   Viva the Diva: Mariah Carey's dressing room demands apparently now includes kittens and puppies

What's going to work for me?

So you might be deciding by now that all I have to do is create some lurid or outrageous headlines and I can kick start my career – be careful that's not always the case.

The Sex Pistols set out to shock and they were hugely aided and abetted by their manager and Svengali, Malcolm McLaren, but the Sex Pistols were the genuine article so it was easy for them to back up the tabloid claims about their anarchic approach to life and music.

I'm guessing that if you're reading this book, you are unlikely to be pursuing a career in punk rock or today's equivalent, but remember that if you do kick start your career with some outrageous stunt you will have to be very comfortable with those early headlines because you are going to be asked about them in every interview you do for the rest of your career.

What I am suggesting you do, however, is to consider what it is about you that can make you stand out in the crowd.

And just to look once again at the exception that proves the rule. It would be hard to imagine more TV exposure and column inches for an artist than those dedicated to Peter Andre and Katie Price over the past couple of years. Although they have both enjoyed some chart success, their record sales to date still bear no relation to their media profile. It's exactly what the Fame Factor's all about; you need a high score in all the categories to make it.

1000 interviews later...

So, let's assume that through a combination of all of your Fame Factor talents and some great publicity you have managed to get well and truly on the road to fame. You have a great manager, a record in the chart and an album full of fantastic songs. By now you will have had quite a lot of experience of the media. You've been on TV and radio and have done lots of magazine interviews; and you sit down with your record company to plan the year ahead.

This must surely be the point when your pop star calendar fills up with world tours, TV specials and, of course, celebrity parties. I have to say that exactly at this point some time in 1988 that I sat down with Kylie Minogue and talked through her schedule for the coming months. She had already had three massive chart hits.

Now Kylie is one of the most professional and hard working artists I have ever had the pleasure of working with, but even she looked at me at that point and said:

"Pete please don't show me a whole month at a time it will just freak me out, just tell me what I'm doing this week!"

So, what was so alarming about the schedule we were proposing? She completed it brilliantly, of course, but it contained day after day of photo shoots, TV appearances and interviews, interviews, interviews. We've already talked about the stamina you need to keep up with those schedules, but here I want to look at how on earth you keep answering the same questions over and over again and make it look like you're saying it for the first time. Something that Kylie is a complete master at.

Of course you think I'm exaggerating when I say 1000 interviews but think about it for a moment. It's quite usual on a promotional tour to do 4 or 5 interviews a day, and when you are starting out as a pop star you can expect to do around 200 days of promotion – and that's just in year one. You do the maths!

Why don't the journalists vary the questions more you may ask? Well some do, but the truth is that when you are starting out, your potential fans are reading about you for the first time and they want to know the basics.

By chance, as I was thinking about this particular Fame Factor, I heard José Carreras (one of the Three Tenors and a world famous opera singer) being interviewed on the radio. The interviewer asked him, "When did you first know you were going to be a singer?"

The 60 year old star told the interviewer his charming story of being taken to the cinema to see a film about the life of Mario Lanza (a legendary opera star). He imbued the story with warmth, enthusiasm and charm and made it sound as if it was the first time an interviewer had ever asked him that question. I wondered just how many times he had told that story in a career that has spanned over four decades.

These days with Katherine Jenkins and Faryl Smith making a strong case for classical music being the new rock and roll, any of you thinking of following in their footsteps should take note of the veteran José Carreras' 'PR'ability' Fame Factor.

Spice Girls get 11 out of 10 for their PR'ability Fame factor

So let's go back to the Spice Girls and why I chose them as the group who would score 11 out of 10 for their 'PR'ability' Fame Factor. Many a political leader would wish that his party members were half as good as the Spice Girls were at staying 'on message'. They had three key planks to their story: Girl Power, the fun they were having as five fantastic friends and their five distinct identities.

No matter how tired they must often have been at trotting out the same lines over and over again in literally thousands of interviews, their enthusiasm and energy was amazing. They bounced, they laughed (Scary shouted quite a lot!), Posh looked demure, Baby was cute, Ginger was bright and Sporty could pull off the odd back flip when required.

All of these elements together generated a massive amount of publicity which was a huge factor in their success. In fact I would go so far as to say that without the media onslaught, 'Wannabe' would never have made the number one spot in 31 countries, and it's doubtful whether the Spice Girls would ever have become a global phenomenon, sold 60 million records worldwide or become the most successful girl group of all time. And would Posh ever have met and married Becks? It's certainly an interesting question.

Spice Girls interview technique...

The Spice Girls invented or were given, it doesn't matter which, a PR story that they clearly believed in and that suited them. They delivered their story with passion, energy and professionalism and in doing so they became the living embodiment of their Girl Power slogan and massive pop stars along the way. There's a lot you can learn about the 'PR'ability' Fame Factor from the start of the Spice Girls' career.

Of course it's a huge help if there are five of you to chip in (see 'Supporting Cast'!) but here's something for you to try. Make a list of the 10 questions you would want to know about your favourite star, but imagine that at this point all you know about them is what they look like and that you love their first record.

Q1

Q2

Q3

Q4

Q5

Q6

Q7

Q8

Q9

Q10

Now imagine that you are that new pop star and think about how you might answer the same questions in the most interesting way and keep the interviewer's and your fans' attention! You can make-up the answers but remember they'll be going into print and you'll be asked the same question over and over!

A1

A2

A3

A4

A5

A6

A7

A8

A9

A10

A Journalist is never your friend

So, having just told you to engage with the journalists, to win them over and get them interested in your story, you must also keep at the back of your mind that a journalist is never your friend.

It's not that they are trying to trip you up or make you say something you will later regret on purpose, but when you are dealing with the tabloid press and the glossy gossip magazines just remember that they have a job to do and 'new singer releases new record' is never going to make the headlines.

Put yourself in their shoes and remember that you need each other, they need the stories and you need the publicity and the most successful artists are the ones who successfully walk this tricky tight rope. Take a look at the array of glossy magazines devoted entirely to celebrity gossip, and then ask yourself how comfortable you would be as the subject of any of those stories. These days it goes with the territory and media coverage is ever more intrusive, but there are a few things you can do to help yourself.

1. Don't say anything about another artist unless you are prepared to see it splashed across one of those magazines. Lily Allen seems to make a particular habit of this but it suits her personality and my guess is that she rarely means what she says but chuckles at the press furore (and publicity!) her outspoken comments create.

2. Get your friends and family to read this chapter. If the magazines can't get anything juicy from you they will often go after those close to you hoping to catch them out in a less media savvy response.

3. Prepare yourself for the fact that however careful you are, you will be misquoted and have something totally innocent taken out of context or given a lurid headline – develop a thick skin when it comes to media coverage and hang on to your sense of humour!

Think I'm exaggerating? Well here are two sample headlines written by journalists based on nothing more than the need to fill a few column inches.

"Kylie is an alien!" One newspaper maintained that she must be an alien as she was too perfect to be human.

"John Lennon's secret message says 'I buried Paul McCartney'". Amid rumours circulating that Paul McCartney was dead, a story ran that if you played 'Strawberry Fields Forever' backwards you could hear John Lennon saying 'I buried Paul'.

Being Papped... Week 52

It's incredibly exciting the first time you step into the glare of the Paparazzi's flash bulbs. However, it's also surprising how soon the novelty fades and that's when you have to find out what works best for you if you really can't handle the thought of being snapped every time you pop out for a paper or a bottle of milk.

I was talking to Girls Aloud's manager Hilary Shaw, just after Cheryl and Kimberley had made it to the top of Kilimanjaro for Comic Relief. An incredible and gruelling undertaking – but the part that you wouldn't be aware of is that while they were being filmed by a sympathetic BBC film crew, they were also being trailed by a couple of paparazzi photographers. You can imagine how this added a whole other layer of difficulty to making your choice of about which bush you are going to hide behind when nature calls half way up a mountain!

However, it can also be a lot easier than some of our beleaguered stars would have us believe to simply go about your business in semi-disguise. A different colour wig, some dark glasses and ordinary clothes will usually do the trick (even the Queen apparently used to pop out to the shops incognito in a head scarf). It's more about a state of mind. If you walk down the street not looking as if you expect everyone to recognise you, most people will just leave you to go about your business. If you jog with a brace of bodyguards, guess what? A paparazzo or two won't be far behind.

Need a bit of publicity? Then get on your designer togs and head to the nearest red carpet event or celebrity restaurant with a hefty security guard or two in tow.

Useful stuff that you can do...

★ Figure out what there is about you that is unique. Is there something about you that will really capture the attention and imagination of your fans?

★ Work out from the start just how much personal information you are prepared to share with the world and how what you say is going to affect your friends and family.

★ Go back to your answers in the interview you created earlier and see whether you can improve on them – are they interesting? Do they contain information you can live with for the rest of your career?

Then rope your friends in to finding some recent interviews in any of the magazines, websites or radio podcasts. Take it in turns to ask each other the same questions. The trick, if you can master it, is to give the interviewer something interesting to write about without you opening the magazine the following week and gasping, "Oh my god did I really say that?"

'Self-Belief' – the most complicated and the most fascinating of all the Fame Factors. To be a successful Pop Star you must have 'Self-Belief', well that's obvious isn't it? How else are you going to survive all the knocks, how else will you talk about yourself endlessly in interviews and step onto a stage in front of 20,000 or even 150,000 people? Yes of course all of my pop icons have 'Self-Belief', they really wouldn't have made it without it, but it's a bit more complicated than that.

You have to believe in yourself or nobody else will. How many times have you heard that from a talent show panel member? It's completely true but sometimes you just need some crucial support and encouragement at the right time and sometimes you need someone to tell you you're getting it hopelessly wrong.

Some artists' deep-seated insecurities allow their nerves to get the better of them, bringing a promising career crashing to the ground before it's even started; others are driven to seek constant affirmation in front of the hugest and most terrifying audiences. Some find the courage to strike out on their own from a successful band; others can't get past the audition to join the band in the first place.

You can be a multi-million selling superstar and still have an incredibly fragile 'Self-Belief'. This Fame Factor is an unreliable ally, one that may disappear at the flimsiest provocation and one that is also capable of unleashing some very destructive demons. I told you it was complicated.

In this chapter I'm going to examine the different aspects of this elusive Fame Factor, I'll take a closer look at the icon who best embodies its complexity, and I'll outline some survival strategies for you to consider.

But let's look first at the positive aspects of 'Self-Belief' and the magical moment when 'a star is born'.

A star is born...

It's one of the most clichéd and overused phrases, especially since we all know that a star is never actually born overnight. They may well suddenly come to the public's attention but it will be after dozens of rejections and years of sheer hard slog spent honing their talent. However, the phrase is so enduring because it does actually describe a moment I have witnessed myself many times.

It's the tipping point when a young artist suddenly takes that crucial step up to real stardom. The moment when the last traces of self-doubt turn into total 'Self- Belief'; it may be only a fleeting moment but it's also a pivotal one.

I have literally seen artists, who were obviously good enough to be signed up to a record company in the first place, suddenly blossom into something bigger and better before your very eyes as they riseto a particular challenge. A live audience will often be the catalyst that makes this happen, hence the prevalence of the phrase in first night reviews; but it can also be the moment they do their first live television appearance or a combination of the two, say on a live talent show. I witnessed exactly that with Will Young on Pop Idol.

Will Young is a very successful solo artist but he is still probably best known for the moment on the first series of Pop Idol when he stood up to Simon Cowell. Simon had called one of his performances 'distinctly average', though the audience, myself included, clearly didn't agree with him. Will remained cool and polite and told Simon, without a trace of arrogance but with total 'Self-Belief', "I don't think you could ever call that average."

Will gave many great performances on the series but for me his 'star is born' moment was when he sang Aretha Franklin's 'Until You Come Back To Me'. The song suited his voice perfectly and it still makes the hairs on the back of my neck stand up just thinking about it.

Robbie Williams – The Ego Has Landed…

Robbie Williams is the icon I have chosen to best represent 'Self-Belief' as he so clearly embodies both sides of this fascinating conundrum. This is the man who can fill the Milton Keynes Bowl with ecstatic fans for a concert broadcast totally live on TV. The band member who had the courage to leave Take That at the height of their success and crow about outstripping their haul of Brit Awards by eleven to four. Surely this artist should have reinforced, rock-solid 'Self- Belief'?

Yet acres of newsprint, much of it vastly overstated but based in truth, have been devoted to Robbie's self-confessed 'demons'. He is also the man who was booked into a clinic for drug abuse by Elton John, was suffering from depression at the height of Take That's fame and has reportedly battled substance abuse, alcoholism and self-esteem issues all his life. Robbie is a funny guy but one reason for his comparative lack of success in America may be his self deprecating wry sense of humour. Who else would name an album and tour 'The Ego Has Landed'?

When Robbie talks about the room where he checks out the internet, he says, "I should not call it my office. I should call it my adulation top-up room!" But he hits it right on the head when he talks about the paradox of an artist's state of mind and says, "This is the wrong business to be in if you are sensitive… but the trouble is – you only get into this business because you are sensitive."

(http://www.bbc.co.uk/stoke/robbie/biog/quotes.shtml)

The biggest high in the world…

It's another cliché but it must be true because every performing artist you ever talk to will tell you that performing in front of a huge crowd who are singing your songs back at you is simply the biggest high in the world. It may be true but this is another fascinating tangle of 'Self-Belief' mixed up with the unique energy provided by a live audience.

I mentioned audience reaction before when I talked about a star being 'born'. It must be remembered that a live audience can also be unforgiving and the reaction an artist gets to a mediocre performance is worlds apart from the one that a brilliant performance generates. When an artist gives a great performance they feel the audience reaction immediately. It's a delicate balance between them, and a kind of magic in which the energy flows both ways.

As the audience applause becomes louder and more enthusiastic, the artist's confidence soars and their performance goes up a notch. It's a self-perpetuating circle, intangible but incredibly real, and as the show progresses it gets better and better; it's the reason why live concerts are such a special and often emotional experience for both the artist and audience.

Your lack of 'Self-Belief' may make you doubt the praise you get from the record company and even your manager, but the love you get from a live audience is real and you only get it if you've earned it! It's not surprising that many stars have mistakenly sought to recreate that incredible euphoria offstage with drink or with drugs.

Strategies to nurture and manage 'Self-Belief'…

1. Fighting Demons

There have been so many stories about artists checking themselves into The Priory and other equally prestigious rehabilitation clinics that you might be forgiven for thinking that a session in 'rehab' is just another part of being a successful artist. This isn't helped by Amy Winehouse's brilliant but misleading song of the same name.

The reality is that drug and drink addiction is painful, that it wrecks families and careers and ultimately will kill you if you don't escape its clutches; just don't go there! You might take stuff in the first place to feel better about yourself but you won't feel better about yourself for very long and you might find yourself having a very public meltdown like Shane Lynch from Boyzone on the MTV awards or having your head shaved in a barber's shop window like Britney.

2. Belief in yourself, but test your talent in public…

Test yourself and your talent. It's no good just singing into your hairbrush in the bedroom, sooner or later you're going to have to perform live in front of an audience so do so as quickly as you can via any available route: local talent shows, school concerts, a solo in the choir. You will know from the reaction of the audience whether you are on the right track.

But remember not to get complacent and to keep stretching yourself; just because you won the sack race when you were eight does not mean you are going to win an Olympic medal at eighteen.

3. Stage Fright

Everyone gets stage fright, it's only natural and it's often a vital part of delivering a great performance. However, once again it's that delicate balance between losing control of your limbs and vocal chords in the worst case scenario, or experiencing a manageable level of stage fright that sets your adrenalin racing and notches your performance up a gear or two.

One way to keep it manageable is to keep pushing yourself and setting yourself challenges. It is far less likely to strike in a destructive way if you have built up a reserve of confidence because you know you have successfully delivered the performance before.

At the other end of this scale I have a personal theory about some of the tantrums and demands we read about from the biggest stars. If it's your 500th live arena show or your 200th live TV appearance, it clearly just cannot generate the same levels of nervous adrenalin as your first. My theory is that some of these temperamental stars may be attempting, consciously or subconsciously, to recreate the earlier tension and fear. If it isn't there naturally then they do something to manufacture it because it's a necessary part of delivering a great performance.

4. Be prepared

The best possible strategy for remaining on the right side of debilitating stage fright is to be as prepared as possible; I touched on it just now. If you are fully rehearsed, have checked out the microphone and monitor mix at the sound check, have tested your outfit and know that it will stand up to the rigours of your dance routine, you will be so much more confident than if you are even slightly unsure about any of these elements.

We made several records with Mandy Smith in the eighties; after the scandal of her relationship with ageing Rolling Stone Bill Wyman had hit the headlines and before she married him. We had hits with her in Europe and Japan. Mandy was gorgeous, one of the most beautiful people inside and out that I've had the pleasure to work with, but when we first started to manage her she had one slightly annoying habit which was to ask unusually detailed questions about any performance we wanted to put into her schedule.

After a while she began to trust that we weren't going to put her into a situation that she wasn't comfortable with or ready for; and then she admitted why she was so paranoid. Her previous manager had booked her a performance in Japan and when she arrived she discovered that the venue was an ice rink, and it got worse. As she gamely wobbled out onto the ice, she realised with horror that the track playing on the PA wasn't the 7" single version but the eight minute 12" remix – of which over half was instrumental! She was left with a live microphone and nothing to do in the middle of an ice rink for over half the record. No wonder then that she wanted to know every last detail of her promo schedule.

5. Don't become immune to criticism...

The more famous you become the more people will be queuing up to tell you how wonderful you are and a strange thing begins to happen. The more praise you receive the less able you become to take any kind of criticism at all. None of us ever like to be criticised, but a big part of becoming successful is to learn from our mistakes and to improve by taking advice from the professionals.

However, even when you reach the heights you will still need objective advice. It might be on the best way to approach an interview on a new TV show, whether the set design you want is practical and affordable or whether your vocals were slightly off because you were partying the night before. You must make sure you have a few people around you who you trust and who will tell you the truth. So many stars surround themselves with 'yes men or women', and this is where a good manager who tells it like it is can be worth their weight in gold. (See also Fame Factor 8 – Supporting Cast)

And finally...

Don't let 'Self-Belief' become self-deception...

There was a famous occasion when Simon Cowell dismissed an X Factor contestant because she was singing out of tune. The girl's parents were spitting feathers and dying to put him right but when Simon came across them in the green room, he was characteristically frank. He told them to take a good look at themselves because they were the reason the girl was so disappointed; they should never have encouraged her to believe she was good enough to make it and that it was cruel to have given her such false hopes.

The poor girl wasn't alone, I have sat through literally thousands of auditions and you just keep asking yourself the question, 'how on earth did they think they were good enough?'

This whole book is about getting you to be realistic about your talents; it's great TV watching some poor young artist making a hash of an audition but with a bit more preparation she still might not have made it, but at least she could have walked away with her head held high knowing she had given it her best shot.

SUPPORTING CAST

Every star needs this Fame Factor, no question about it, you simply can't progress without it and the bigger you get, the bigger your 'Supporting Cast' will become. In this chapter I look at two different types of Supporting cast – one is optional, the other is not.

1. The 'Supporting Cast' provided by your fellow group members and the pros and cons of being a solo artist versus a member of a group.

2. Your professional 'Supporting Cast': your manager, agent, promoter, production team, security etc.; all of the people that you will need at different stages of your career.

Of course if you are lucky you will also have a 'Supporting Cast' provided by family and friends and I will talk about this as well, but in this chapter I will mainly talk about the first two. I shall also provide you with some helpful facts and information, and highlight some career choices you may not have yet considered. I also get a couple of insights from two of the music industry's top managers: Hilary Shaw, Girls Aloud's manager, and Terry Blamey who has managed Kylie's career for over twenty years.

Although all of my featured artists have great professional 'Supporting Casts', (remember this is a Fame Factor you really cannot do without) I picked Girls Aloud as the perfect artists to illustrate this Fame Factor because they have both types of 'Supporting Cast' in spades. They have a fantastic professional team behind them and have done right from the start, and Cheryl, Nadine, Nicola, Sarah and Kimberley have been a brilliant 'Supporting Cast' for each other as members of one of Britain's most successful girl groups.

You might think that winning any major TV talent show would be a guaranteed passport to success. Not so, I haven't done the exact figures, but for every Will Young (Pop Idol 2002), Leona Lewis (X Factor 2006) or indeed Girls Aloud (Popstars: The Rivals 2002), there are almost as many Steve Brooksteins (X Factor 2004), Michelle McManuses (Pop Idol 2003) or David Sneddons (Fame Academy 2002).

Girls Aloud have been the most successful to date, remaining consistently in the charts, in the media and in huge arenas filled with devoted fans. Since their first single 'Sound of the Underground' claimed the number one slot, Girls Aloud have enjoyed a straight run of twenty consecutive hit singles, and there's a very good reason for that.

Of course they are talented, but they also have a brilliant professional team around them. Their record company and managers made sure they had great songs and made great records by working with the right record producers and songwriters. Then their managers, agents and promoters carefully built up their live appearances and tours until they were where they are today, selling out massive arenas.

Later in this chapter we will look at the professionals you are going to need in your 'Supporting Cast' at each stage of your career. I'll give you a broad outline of the jobs they should perform, the qualities you should look for in them, who pays them and roughly how much.

I've talked to Terry Blamey (Kylie's manager) and asked him to give his personal view of the vital qualities required for the job, then checked out Kylie's take on their relationship.

However, for starters let's go back and take a look at the support you might expect and enjoy being a member of a group. Girls Aloud are a great example of how well a group can work together, backing each other up on stage and in the media. Can you imagine how much fun they had, particularly in the early days, having a bunch of girlfriends to share the highs and more importantly to support each other through the lows.

United we stand, divided we fall...

Girls Aloud have been together for seven successful years now, which is almost a record, considering the pop industry is littered with artists who thought they could do better on their own. In many cases they left successful groups for limited success or worse, relative obscurity. Even the most successful girl group in the world – The Spice Girls – could never get close to the same level of success with any of their solo careers as they had achieved together as a group.

After leaving Westlife and a run of 11 number one hits, Bryan McFadden's solo career soon waned. Rachel Stevens was the only one of S Club 7 to have real solo success, but again it doesn't compare to her former band's achievements and none of Steps have reached the same heights as solo pop stars since the band split up.

All of the Beatles had success after their acrimonious split and produced classic solo records such as John Lennon's 'Imagine', George Harrison's 'My Sweet Lord' and Paul McCartney's 'Jet', but their solo hits are vastly outnumbered and outclassed by the sheer volume and creativity of the groundbreaking Beatles catalogue. With successful pop groups it is so often the case that the whole is usually much greater than its individual parts.

Those who achieve similar or even more success as a solo artist are few and far between; although there are always exceptions that prove the rule and two of the best examples I can think of are Robbie Williams and Justin Timberlake.

Robbie Williams achieved superstardom after quitting Take That in a dramatic and reportedly drug fuelled resignation. He then rose from the ashes of the almost defunct band he left behind to release his first solo album 'Life Thru a Lens' which contained the classic 'Angels' and his signature tune 'Let Me Entertain You'. He went on to sell 55 million records worldwide and to win 11 Brit awards (to add to the paltry 4 that he had won with Take That!).

When the members of NSYNC decided to take a break as a group and pursue solo projects it was Justin Timberlake who emerged as the global superstar. They are the exceptions; however, you shouldn't run away with the idea that life after a career as the member of a hit band is all drugs, depression, and appearances in second rate reality shows. The various members of NSYNC, for instance, went on to be successful writers, actors and even, I kid you not, a NASA certified Cosmonaut! And Take That came back for a massively successful reunion tour in 2008 with some new hits penned by Gary Barlow, an Ivor Novello award for 'Shine' and a Brit Award for 'Best British Live Act'.

Now you may already have very firm ideas about the route you are going to take and whether your best chance of success lies in pursuing a solo career or as a member of a group. All I will suggest is that you keep an open mind until you've had a look at the next few pages where I consider the options against some of the Fame Factors we've discussed; then try the personality test that follows.

Band member vs. solo artist
– pitfalls and advantages…

Supporting Cast

The road to success as you're beginning to see (and probably had some idea of before you opened this book) is a hard one. It requires great stamina and determination and is bound to have major disappointments along the way. Being in a band means that you will be able to share the incredible highs as well as the devastating lows with three or four other people. You are all in the same boat and can support each other.

It can be lonely being a solo artist on the road, especially at the beginning of your career and it's very unlikely that, with the best will in the world, your friends and family will quite understand just what you are going through. However, you are going to spend a ridiculous amount of time together as a group and sooner or later you will start to get on each other's nerves, it's only human nature.

As a solo artist once you've made it you can choose who's in the tour bus and who's on stage with you. But remember that a supporting cast of employees may not be as frank and truthful as fellow band members and take a look at the final section of this chapter on 'Friends and Family'.

PR-ability

You've now got some idea of the daunting promotional schedule you'll be asked to follow in your first couple of years and although you will probably all have to turn up for the same interviews, presenting a united front, sharing the load when it comes to those relentlessly repeated questions has definite advantages.

However, inevitably one or two of the group will be better at this and this can lead to boredom and resentment from the band members who are reduced to sitting on the sofa looking pretty. As a solo artist you will have sole responsibility for answering those endlessly repeated questions but you won't have to worry about another band member doing or saying something stupid and you will always be the one in the headlines.

Distinctive Voices and Killer Moves

Being in a group allows you to capitalise on each others' strengths, letting the best voices take the lead in the studio and in live performances while the best dancers dazzle the audience with their fancy footwork. Take That are a perfect example of this strategy.

It is so obvious it almost sounds silly to write this, but a group's record producers will always allocate the lion's share of the lead vocals to the best singers in the group, but it's incredible how quickly this can also start to build jealousy and dissatisfaction. When the weaker singers start demanding their turn at the lead vocals, the band's producers and songwriters start nursing major headaches as they try to write around their vocal shortcomings. As a solo artist the lead vocals are all yours, every day (including, of course, the days you are dog-tired and have a sore throat!).

The Look

The visual impact of five performers, especially when their look is coordinated, is often greater than that of a solo artist. It's much easier to fill the stage and it gives the cameras more angles and interesting shots to go for.

As a group you may be completely united on the styling front, but it is much more likely that one or two of you will not be mad about band's 'Look'. Not everyone can copy the Spice Girls with five different looks and personas, and you may find yourself performing on national TV in an outfit that you would really rather not be wearing. As a solo artist you can decide (with your advisors and stylists) what works for you without having to worry about fitting in with the rest of the group.

Public Appeal

A group can increase its chances of succeeding and keeping a big fan base as the different members are likely to appeal to different fans even without the Spice Girls' device of deliberately picking five very different looks and personalities. Every Take That and Westlife fan has their favourite band member.

As a solo artist you will not have to share the spotlight, the cameras or the adulation of the crowd with anyone, this also means that the pressure to deliver a perfect performance every single time remains squarely on your shoulders.

Money

For all its other advantages I can think of no financial advantage to being a member of a group over being a solo artist. However, you should weigh this up against your chances of success in the first place and whether you are more likely to make it as a member of a group or as a solo artist.

Everything the band earns has to be split four or five ways depending on the number of people in the band. Even if you don't write your own material, as a solo artist you are going to be quids in as you get to keep the lot after expenses and commissions have been deducted (with the exception of writing royalties – see Fame Factor 1 – 'The Songs').

However, let me say here and now that if getting rich is your main motivation then put this book down now and look for another career; to make it as a successful pop star you need to be passionate about performing, not making money!

QUIZ – Solo or Spice Girl

I know there's a lot to consider so if you're still confused, answer these questions as honestly as possible then see how you rate as a potential solo artist or group member.

1. **You have made it through to the final 10 in the search for the new Girls Aloud but there's one slight problem. You love your amazing waist length, naturally platinum blond hair, but the remaining vacancy is for a cropped red head. Do you:**
a) Don't even think twice about the makeover, this is your big opportunity?
b) Try to talk the show producers into letting you keep your hair by convincing one of the other blonds in the line up to go for the colour and crop?
c) Refuse to compromise your look?

2. **You've been booked to sing on the pitch of your local city's football club at the start of the season. The acoustics are horrible so the plan is that you will lip synch (mime) to the record. However, the tour manager has gone AWOL and you are there with no CD and a ropey microphone. Do you:**
a) Sing acapella (unaccompanied vocals) with the ropey microphone, wow the crowd (and sack the tour manager)?
b) Explain to the crowd that you don't have a backing track, tell them you'll be back the following week and in the meantime you'll be available in the bar to sign as many autographs as they want (and sack the tour manager)?
c) Sack the tour manager and get the club manager to tell the crowd you are stuck on the motorway and can't make it?

3. You're going to be stranded on a desert island for 3 months. You will be given food and drink supplies but can only take one luxury item with you. Will it be:

a) Your Ipod? You couldn't be without your music.

b) Your mobile phone? You couldn't go without talking to anyone for 3 months!

c) Your make-up/hair gel? In case there happens to be a handsome Man/Woman Friday on the island.

4. Your producer has promised you lead vocals on the new record if you can convince the rest if the band to come to his 6 year olds birthday party. Do you:

a) Agree and start planning how you're going to get the band there without telling them why?

b) Confide in the band and hope that they let you sing the next lead vocal anyway? It's your turn and you know you are good enough.

c) Do nothing? You don't believe the choice of vocalist is up to him anyway.

5. It's your first photo session with a top photographer and the stylist is set on shocking pink ensembles that clash horribly with your skin tone. Do you:

a) Get to the studio slightly ahead of the others so that you can at least make sure you get the most flattering outfit?

b) Trust that the make-up artist is clever enough to make you look good?

c) Try to convince the stylist that there is time to get a different look?

6. You are terrified of heights and Comic Relief have asked you to do a sponsored tandem skydive for the charity. Do you:

a) Say yes and focus on the amazing publicity it will create?

b) Say yes as long as the rest of the band will do it with you for moral support?

c) Offer to do something less spectacular but also less terrifying?

7. It's the morning after a really big night out on an exhausting promo trip and you wake up with a jolt remembering that you

promised to go shopping with a friend to find her prom dress and you're due to meet her in half an hour. Do you:

a) Struggle into your clothes and text her to tell her you'll be ten minutes late?

b) Call her, apologise profusely and talk her into going the following day?

c) Turn off your phone and crawl back under the duvet, you are exhausted and your friend will understand?

8. Your record company has hired an amazing choreographer for your next video and you are worried that your fellow band members are going to outshine you. Do you:

a) Go for it, he's not going to make you look an idiot?

b) Go for it, if he's that good he'll make the overall video look amazing?

c) Lose sleep the night before so that the make-up artist has to find extra highlighter for the dark circles under your eyes?

Mostly A's...

You certainly think you have the confidence and determination to make it on your own without the safety blanket of a group to share the limelight. You are happy with your own company and abilities and if you have high scores in least 7 or more of the Fame Factors – the solo route could be the one for you

Mostly B's...

You like sharing and having your friends around you and could flourish as a member of a group. For this you need loyalty and a degree of patience and diplomacy which you also appear to have. You may also think that your fellow band members will bolster your Fame Factor weak points

Mostly C's...

Are you sure that the pop business is really for you? You don't appear to have the self-belief or determination to make it on your own and you also seem to lack the loyalty to be part of a group

Supporting Cast – The Professionals

I am sure that most of you are familiar with the names of the people who form the close circle around a pop star. Here we look at the nuts and bolts of what they actually do and the percentages you should expect to pay the key people.

The Manager

It's the manager's job to make all your business deals including your record deal, to employ the rest of your professional 'Supporting Cast' and to make sure that everybody is doing the best possible job for you. Your manager is the key person responsible for making the decisions that can make or break your career so choose him or her wisely.

They filter all the offers that come in and approve the record company promotion schedules. They have the experience to decide on your behalf whether a promo trip to a new territory may be more valuable to you in the long run than a fee paying gig in the UK. Above all they are looking out for your health and welfare, pushing you when they know it's in your best interests but ensuring that you are not completely overworked (although this may be hard to remember when your alarm call comes at 5 in the morning!).

Since you will be paying this person around 20% of your gross income to provide you with their expert advice, you had better choose someone with either a great track record or someone as ambitious as you who has a great business brain and is a very quick learner. (Your gross income means the record company advances, performance fees and royalties you receive before expenses, commissions and taxes have been deducted.) If you really make it big, they will be dealing with very large sums of money. A good manager will always have your best interests at the centre of every decision he or she makes.

Brian Epstein, the manager of The Beatles, had the connections through his family's electrical goods business to get four lads from Liverpool a deal with Parlophone Records, part of EMI. The jury is still out, depending on which book you read, as to whether he was a great manager or not. One thing is for sure, he cared deeply about the band, did the best job he was able to and without that introduction to EMI and producer George Martin it's entirely possible that The Beatles might never have made it.

Hilary Shaw joined Girls Aloud as their manager once they had already had some success. The girls had been managing themselves for a while but when they needed help putting their first major UK tour together, they turned to Hilary. She was an established manger with an impressive track record and there is very little she doesn't know about managing a girl group having been Bananarama's manager throughout their biggest successes. I asked her what are the top three qualities you should look for in a manager?

HS: Experience, reliability and good people skills and above all you have to have a complete understanding of all areas of the music industry

PW: What's the best thing about being a manager?

HS: Usually I am working with an artist for a long time before it is presented to the public. I put my heart and soul into it and it's incredibly rewarding when it's received well and you end up with a hit record.

PW: And the worst?

HS: Not being able to take a relaxing holiday as they have to be working holidays. It's a 24/7 business.

PW: How many requests a week do you get for the girls?

HS: I get hundreds of requests that come via Fascination or direct to me

PW: How many of them are worth considering?

HS: You could count them on one hand.

Many of the most successful artists have had the same manager from day one. Terry Blamey has been with Kylie for over 20 years. Ask any manager of a successful act and you will be amazed by the number of offers they get every week. As Hilary said she gets hundreds of requests from TV propositions to film scripts to opening the local fete or endorsing a can of dog meat. So I asked Terry what he thought the formula for a good relationship was and how on earth he sifted through all those requests. He said:

"The secret to a successful partnership, between artist and manager, is all about respect and trust. It is essential that you have respect for each other and have faith in each other's skills. You must also be able to trust each other; the artist has to be confident that the manager always has their best interests at the forefront of any decision. The decision making process consists of three questions, in this order:

1. Is this something my artist would want to do or, at worst, wouldn't mind doing?

2. Will this enhance the artist's career or, at worst, do the career no harm whatsoever?

3. Is this financially viable?

A strong "no" at any stage results in a negative decision."

Kylie clearly has a amazing team of people around her, and in a Music Week interview she was asked about her 'Supporting Cast' keeping pace with her ever changing vision for her look and her shows. They asked:

"All that change and versatility is counteracted by a handful of long-standing business relationships, particularly with your manager, Terry Blamey. Do you think that's helped your creative side?" And she responded:

"Absolutely. Terry and I came back on the Eurostar from Paris recently and I just thought 'Oh my God, I remember us being on the Bullet Train going from Tokyo to God-knows-where and all the situations we've been in where he'll say things that either crack me up or... disturb me [laughs]."

Music Week special supplement
for 'Ultimate Kylie',
dated 27/11/2004

The Record Company

We're going to look in a minute at the vast machine that rolls into gear for a major tour, but before we get ahead of ourselves let's remember that before you get that far you're going to need some hit records and for that you're going to need a record company.

With free downloads and piracy rampant, the record companies have been having a hard time of it of late, however let's look at the basic principles of the model that has worked and will continue to work for the more successful artists.

The record company signs you to the label for a set amount of time (usually for five years with the options on their side) and if you're hot property they will pay you an advance. They then foot the bill to record and manufacture your CD's, or make downloads available. They also pay the record producers and all the marketing costs: employing PR agents and record 'pluggers', running ads and making videos. And while you are making those videos and TV appearances they will be hiring and paying for the stylists, choreographers, rehearsals, make-up artists and vocal coaches, not to mention video directors and art designers.

All of which adds up to a hefty bill (somewhere in the region of a million pounds) which they will recoup from their share of the record royalties. You, by the way, will only receive royalties once the record company has recouped the advance they paid you to sign to the label.

Record companies so often get a bad press from disgruntled artists complaining about a lack artistic freedom whilst completely overlooking the fact that it is usually the record company's expertise that has made them successful in the first place. Ninety-nine times out of a hundred it is the record company's money that has funded the artist's career so they are perfectly justified in wanting a say in how that career develops.

The relationship between the artist and record label can be a tricky one to negotiate (another job for the manager), even the name 'music business' suggests potential for conflict as creativity and commerce are always likely to clash. But it has also proved to be an excellent and mutually beneficial partnership for thousands of artists since the beginning of pop music.

The Record Producer / Songwriter

Unless your record company is like my company PWL with in-house writers and producers, the record company will decide on and hire your record producer and the songwriters they think you should work with. See also Fame Factor 1 – The Songs.

Quite simply the Record Producer's job is to make a great record and this will always involve getting the best vocal performances from the artist, and overseeing the musical arrangement, style and sound of the track. With a pop record this will usually involve booking the musicians who will provide the musical backing track. Stock Aitken Waterman wrote, produced and usually played on all our own records and had an incredible track record – a record in the charts every week of the year for 4 years with a 17 number ones.

The Publisher

You will only need a music publisher if you write your own material – see also Fame Factor 1 – The Songs, where I look at the creative role of a music publisher. In very simple terms your publisher will collect your publishing royalties for a percentage of your income. Publishing is a complex area of the business and my counsel here is to make sure you have proper legal advice before agreeing a deal and don't think that you can manage your own publishing to avoid giving a publisher their percentage.

The Video Director/Producer

When the record company needs a video to promote a single release they will usually ask several well-known video production companies and/or directors to submit treatments and storyboards with ideas for the video. Sometimes the artist will have an input in this although for a pop act in its early stages this is rare; remember the record company is paying for the video which these days could cost anything from £15,000 to £150,000 – (although the budget for extravaganzas like Thriller probably ran close to half a million dollars even back in the early 1980's).

The Stylist, Hair and Make-up

We talked about what 'the Glam squad' actually do in Fame Factor 3 – The Look. Suffice it to say that once again the record company will be footing the bill, so will have the final choice in the early stages of your career as to who you work with. However, since their aim is for you to look as good as possible, artists often like and trust the people their record company introduces them to and sometimes go on to work with them for many years. Once you start to tour, you will need to hire and pay for this section of your supporting cast yourself together with all of your touring personnel.

The Choreographer

The man or woman hired by you or your record company to create the dance routines for your videos, TV performances and live shows. Even if it is essentially the same routine it will still need to be reworked and adapted for each type of performance and the available space. They will also choreograph your backing dancers. See also Fame Factor 9 – Killer Moves.

The Agent

Your agent makes the deals on your behalf for all your paying performances, either directly with the venues in the early stages of your career or with a promoter once you get to the larger shows and tours. They have relationships with all the venue owners and promoters and know exactly how to get you the highest fee from which they will make a 10% commission fee (once again from the gross income).

The Promoter

The Promoter is the one who promotes, i.e. advertises and markets your shows. They sell the tickets and, depending on the stature of the artist, agree a guaranteed fee with the artist's agent (or sometimes the manager) before the tickets go on sale. Although these days most promoters are tied in with big corporations like Live Nation and AEG, who also control most of the major music venues, a promoter has to be something of a gambler. They study the band's form, gauge what price to charge for the tickets and how to make the accounts balance enough to pay the artist and make a profit.

Even though a band is selling out arenas, as the touring production costs are so expensive this still remains a precarious way to make a living despite the continuing popularity of live music. Knowing whether to book 2 or 3 nights at the 02 Arena in London can easily mean the difference between a healthy profit or a substantial loss. I suspect that the financial fallout from the fifty cancelled shows that Michael Jackson was due to play at London's 02 Arena this summer (2009) will be rumbling on for several years to come.

The Production Manager

At the start of your career, if you are playing tiny gigs, it's quite likely that your manager will perform all of the roles he or she will later allocate to a Production Manager and Tour Manager, as the calls on the manager's time become ever more demanding and complex. But let's jump straight ahead to the 'Supporting Cast' you're going to need to pull off a massive arena tour.

The Production Manager is an impressive character, they are the Kings (or Queens) of a small empire and manage budgets worth millions of pounds. If you ever have the chance to see a George Michael or Elton John production, roll in overnight to a massive stadium or arena and you'll see it's a scarily awesome operation and one that employs hundreds of technicians and crew.

The Production Manager is responsible for the safety of his crew; the audience and not least of course, you the artist! As Take That strode across the heads of the audience on their bridge to the B stage in the middle of the Arena on their 2007 Comeback Tour, or Girls Aloud track across the arena on their moving overhead platform, you are also looking at several tons of metal that the Production Manager has overseen from its initial concept with the designer, through to its transportation and eventual construction and dismantling night after night.

He has agreed the lighting design and the positioning of up to 500 individual lamps including the rigging installed to support them (more tons of steel) and the position and quality of the sound system. He hires the riggers, the sound and lighting technicians and the people who design and build the set on stage which almost always includes a variety of enormous moving LED screens. He also employs the teams who create and control the images that go onto those screens including the cameras that relay giant pictures of the band.

George Michael's '25 Live' tour involved a set design comprising almost entirely of a gigantic wave of LED screen that rolled over and off the front of the stage, a challenging engineering feat on its own without needing to be transported to a different city every few days. Major tours will often have replica sets, trucks and crews who piggy back between dates as it's the only way to logistically provide for back to back dates in different cities – George's tour had two identical screens doing exactly that.

The Tour Manager

Earlier in your touring career, whilst the production is more manageable, the Production Manager may also be the Tour Manager. However, by the time your show production starts to grow, you will usually need a separate Tour Manager. His or her job is to take care of the artist's schedule on the road and all their transport arrangements. He will be the one looking harassed in the hotel lobby, trying to find a missing sound engineer so the tour bus can leave on time. He will settle the hotel bills, issue everyone with itineraries and liaise with the band's drivers.

The Tour Manager is likely to work more closely with the artists on a day to day basis. Since a show day may also involve a TV interview or a meet and greet with the fans, the Tour Manager is the one who will often oversee this in place of the manager.

The Security Manager

You've all seen the Mariah Carey style security, flanking the artist 6 deep and bristling with muscles, dark glasses and possibly firearms shoulder-holstered under their Armani jackets. This level of security is rarely necessary and is definitely not required on a daily basis, but there are occasions when you need some personal security and this is what they should do.

They are there, of course, for your protection, but from what? From a lunatic who hurls themselves at you in an attempt to steal a kiss (rarely anything worse) or from the sheer volume of fans when you are trying to leave a show. Often this will entail bundling you into your limo just seconds after you have left the stage so that you are safely on the road before the fans can even think about swamping the stage door. Chances are he will have found an alternative exit anyway as he will have checked all the available safe entrances and exits. Apart from Kevin Costner (in the film The Bodyguard) I have never heard of a security person actually taking a bullet for their client! The best personal security person is the one that is vigilant and prepared, but also able to merge into the background.

Several hits into her career Kylie appeared on my 'Hitman And Her' show in Blackpool. The stage was tiny and totally unsuitable for an appearance of a star of her stature. On this occasion the security person we had hired for her was Jerry Judge. Jerry has looked after hundreds of pop stars and A-list actors; he fits into the blending into the background category, but is six-foot and quite strong enough to pick Kylie up with one arm.

He told her firmly that he was drawing an imaginary line across the front of the stage that would keep her just out of reach of the fans. He told her that if she put just one foot over it – the next thing she would feel would be his arm around her scooping her back. She grinned at me and winked and said "it would almost be worth it!"

The Driver

You might wonder what there is to say about the man who drives the car, but a pop star's driver belongs to an interesting breed and needs more skills than you might at first think. Number one is total loyalty and discretion unless you intend never to bitch about anyone, snog anyone or have just a little too much to drink before you get into the car – you see what I mean.

He or she must be an exceptional driver and skilled at getting you out of some tricky situations especially when, after the best laid plans, your car ends up surrounded by screaming fans and he must extricate the car without injuring anyone. He or she may also double-up as security when required.

A great driver will know when you are in the mood to talk and when to keep it completely zipped. Tony Laurie looked after me and all the PWL artists for years and believe me, I speak from experience when I say that when you land back at Heathrow after a gruelling promotional tour there is nothing better than being met by a familiar and utterly reliable face. A good driver is worth their weight in gold.

Supporting Cast – Family and Friends

I've left it till last because obviously there's nothing like the support of family and friends, the ones who loved you before you were famous and will love you if it all disappears. If you're really lucky and you put some effort into it, these can be your rock.

I say if you put some effort into it, because I've said it before but adoration is a heavy and intoxicating drug and one which often renders the recipient totally incapable of receiving criticism from anyone – not even their nearest and dearest.

This can become even more complicated when a parent becomes the artist's manager which, in my opinion, is hardly ever a good idea as that it rarely works for the following reasons:

1) The parent rarely has the required skills and expertise.

2) The parent is usually too close to their son or daughter to be objective. Remember Simon Cowell's outburst at the X Factor parents?

As ever there are exceptions that prove the rule. Matthew Knowles managed Beyoncé until fairly recently and clearly did an amazing job. However, we are also aware of the worst excesses of pushy stage parents if all of Michael Jackson's stories about his father terrorising the child star are to be wholly believed.

So my final words on your professional 'Supporting Cast' are these:

★ Get yourself a good manager as soon as you can

★ Listen to them – they have your best interests at heart

★ Remember – Pop stardom also brings a whole clutch of exciting new best friends who will be happy to agree with everything you say just to keep in with you

★ Try to keep a sense of perspective

★ Remain open to constructive criticism

★ Keep in close touch with your real friends and family

At the back of the book there's a list of websites of various organisations that can provide further general advice and information about the 'business' side of your career.

KILLER MOVES

Just as it's vital to have a 'Distinctive Voice' and 'The Look', the Fame Factor that will stamp you indelibly on the publics' consciousness is a set of 'Killer Moves'. My acid test for this Fame Factor is that when you name the artist or the song at least half of any group of people will instantly share the same moving image.

I admit that I am really spoilt for choice when considering pop icons who best illustrate the 'Killer Moves' Fame Factor, but from the moment she appeared on the scene as the lead singer in Destiny's Child, Beyoncé Knowles created a stage presence and a set of moves that made men fall in love with her and women want to be her. Together with some great songs and an amazing voice, Beyoncé's 'Killer Moves' have helped to stake her place at the top of the charts in America and all over the world.

To prove my point, I defy anyone not to hear that brass intro to 'Crazy In Love' and not see the gorgeous Beyoncé striding towards you before executing a perfect 'booty shake'.

If you happen to be a dance genius you can, of course, invent your own choreography – think Michael Jackson and the Moonwalk. Jackson was an incredible dancer, every stage routine and most of his videos had the slickest most exciting choreography, but I can't think of a single move by any other artist that so many people have tried to emulate (with varying degrees of success!).

If you have two left feet and the whole idea of adding dance moves to your performance fills you with dread, don't worry – there are hugely successful artists who have their own solution to this Fame Factor element and we'll look at them later in the chapter. But 'Killer Moves' have been and will continue to be an incredibly important part of a pop artist's repertoire and what I'm going to do here is to identify some successful and very different styles to help you to find work out what might work best for you.

Eight of the Best Killer moves in Pop History

To select these 'Killer Moves' I used a very simple test: if you told a group of ten music fans the names of the following songs and artists, at least half of them would be able to imitate the moves that go with the song.

1. Beyoncé – Crazy In Love
Strong Sexy and Sassy

Every move that Beyoncé Knowles makes on stage proclaims her a superstar. She has chosen simple but effective choreography that is strong, sexy and sassy. Her 'Killer Moves' suit her music and her image perfectly; most importantly they also allow her to deliver her stunning vocal performances. Striding across the stage she out-stalks the supermodels and then moves seamlessly into the Beyoncé 'booty shake'.

The booty shake itself isn't a particularly original piece of choreography. Borrowed from traditional African dance moves it owes a lot to Tina Turner, but Beyoncé proves that a 'Killer Move' doesn't have to be so much about complicated choreography as finding the moves that work for you and stamping your personality on them. If you do you might even get Justin Timberlake in a leotard parodying you on Saturday Night Live.

2. Michael Jackson – Thriller
Creative Choreography Genius

Michael Jackson was one of the first artists to bring a scale of production comparable to a Hollywood Musical to a pop video. Thriller showcases his own brilliant and innovative dancing, but the almost fourteen minute mini epic made for the six minute single also has its own narrative, including a menacing line of shrugging zombies who join one of the most recognisable and most copied dance routines ever. When 1500 orange clad prisoners posted a video on YouTube of their Thriller performance in their Philippine prison yard, complete with its signature choreography, it received 300,000 hits a day and became one of the most watched ever viral videos.

The scale of a Thriller routine may always be beyond your reach but Jackson's vision and those incredible dance skills honed in endless practice rooms should always be a source of inspiration.

3. Village People – Y.M.C.A
Simple but Unforgettable

OK, so we may be going from the sublime to the ridiculous, literally, but you can only argue with this choice if you DON'T know all of the arm movements for 'Y.M.C.A.'! It's on my list to represent a whole clutch of artists and records that were helped to huge chart success by attaching themselves to an easy to learn dance routine. Since Chubby Checker sang 'Let's twist again like we did last summer', artists have been having hit records that rely on a dance that has the ability to capture the public's imagination on the dance floor.

For example, 'The Locomotion', originally performed by Little Eva and then, of course, by Kylie, had people chugging around the dance floor in train formation, and Madness had arenas full of people doing the 'Nutty Boy' take on a Ska Shuffle. Finally the daddy of them all, 'Macarena', was the second longest running number 1 in America and the bestselling debut single of all time. Sadly for its singer Los del Rio, it was also probably the most successful one hit wonder. Make sure you that have a great follow up song if you are considering this type of 'Killer Move'!

4. Madonna – Vogue
Glamourising an existing dance style

Madonna started her career as a dancer so it is no surprise that dance has always played a huge part in her shows and videos, but 'Vogue' remains her most famous set of 'Killer Moves'. It was undeniably a great pop dance record, but if you break it down it is also – shock horror – an incredibly cool, stylised and rather more challenging version of Y.M.C.A!

'Vogueing' originated in the underground clubs in Harlem, New York. Drag queens competed to out-Vogue each other as they portrayed glamorous Hollywood film stars through a series of complicated hand gestures and body shapes. Madonna adapted the moves into her distinctive choreography and demanded that everyone 'strike a pose'. The choreography, together with Madonna's fabulous performance in her classic black and white video, not only helped the record to become a massive crossover hit but also cemented her position as the number one gay icon of the time.

5. Steps – 5,6,7,8
Updating an existing dance style

Country music has never been mainstream in the UK although it has always had an incredibly loyal following. In 1992 Billy Ray Cyrus' huge hit 'Achy Break Heart' introduced line dancing to the UK and it had been steadily growing in popularity by 1998 when Steps brought out '5,6,7,8'. The record set out to shamelessly capitalise on the growing craze but, performed by five sparky, good-looking and talented kids, it took line dancing temporarily out of the village halls and into thousands of little girls' bedrooms as they copied the 'boot scootin'' moves.

I include this as a set of 'Killer Moves' because anyone under the age of 30 will probably start twirling an imaginary lasso in the air and turning in a circle to the refrain of '5,6,7,8'. It's also a great example of taking an old dance style and updating it and it also jump-started Steps' career who followed it up with a series of massive pop hits. Their name of course refers to the fact that dance 'steps' were a huge part of their act, (who can forget 'Tragedy') and a big factor in helping them to have a massively successful career.

6. Bananarama – Venus
Street Glamour

Before Bananarama, girl groups had choreography but it tended to involve nothing more daring than a gentle flick of the wrist and as much synchronised shimmying as their skin hugging sequined glamour gowns would allow. Bananarama's 'Killer Moves' changed all that and set the scene for so many girl groups that followed.

The choreography for Venus, created by Bruno Tonioli (yes he of Strictly Come Dancing fame), took the moves that had been so sedately performed by groups like the Supremes but added a clubby energy and bucket loads of attitude not to mention a chorus of beautiful toy boys and the girls' own cameos as a very sexy devil, a vampire and a Greek goddess. The girls were edgy, unbelievably cool and girls in clubs across the country leapt to the dance floor to emulate their 'Killer Moves' and energy as soon as they heard the opening bars of 'Venus'. Bananarama were all about street fashion and they found 'Killer Moves' to match.

7. New Kids On The Block – Hangin' Tough
Dancing For Boys

OK, I will admit that if you asked a group of pop fans about the 'Hangin' Tough' Killer Moves you might get nothing more ambitious than a load of energetic arm waving and overhead clapping, but New Kids on the Block are generally considered the first of a long and successful stream of dancing Boy Bands, making it cool for boys to dance.

The 'Hangin' Tough' video was set in graffiti covered alleys and showcased the boys dance credentials with their edgy, athletic hip hop influenced moves. Go back and look at it; it was made in 1988 and you'll be amazed at how current it looks. NKOB raised the bar for Boy Bands – suddenly you had to dance as well as sing. They were followed by the likes of Take That, Backstreet Boys, East 17 and NSYNC. Had it not been for the success of 'Hangin' Tough', Robbie Williams and Justin Timberlake might never have become the stars they are today and George Sampson and Diversity might never have won the second and third series of Britain's Got Talent.

8. Kylie – Can't Get You Out Of My Head
Making 'Killer Moves' look so simple

There are so many Kylie songs I could have chosen from 'Hand On Your Heart' to 'Better the Devil You Know' and all the way through to her spectacular Show Girl Tour. I decided eventually that 'Can't Get You Out of My Head' would induce the most synchronised shoulder shrugging from the greatest number of people and it perfectly illustrates marrying the dance style to the music – something that Kylie has done brilliantly throughout her career.

Kylie inherited her natural dance talent from her mum and I always remember the first time we put together a routine with dancers for 'Locomotion' for Top of the Pops. As ever at that early stage in her pop career she was only able to take short breaks from her 'Neighbours' filming schedule so we hoped that the two day rehearsal would be enough for her; the dancers had taken two days and they were professionals. Kylie arrived, somewhat jet-lagged, straight off the overnight plane from Melbourne; by lunchtime she had the routine down and by mid afternoon it was perfect. If you have a god given talent like Kylie you have so many more possibilities so just make sure that your 'Killer Moves' are in tune with the music.

Your Killer Moves

So now that you have looked afresh at the range of 'Killer Moves' at your disposal you should make your own list of favourites and really look at what makes each of them work for that artist. My selection is not, of course, the definitive list, that's the whole point of being a creative artist and coming up with something original!

Remember too that very few people actually have Kylie's natural talent or Michael Jackson's dance genius; most people simply have to work *very* hard at it. Watching Girls Aloud on their recent arena tour it was easy to forget that when they first fought for their places in Girls Aloud on 'Popstars The Rivals' they weren't all brilliant dancers, a fact that you forget entirely when you see them slinking across the stage in perfect formation (and how do they do that in those heels!).

Girls Aloud have benefited from the help of top choreographers who cleverly play to their strengths. You are unlikely to have access to such expertise, but dance lessons will always be a great investment for general fitness and helping you to pick up any style of choreography in the future. Even if you can't afford expensive lessons, you can always learn your favourite dance routines from the millions of videos in circulation on the web these days.

However, if all these options have left you reeling let me summarise for you. Your personal 'Killer Moves' should:

★ Be easily identifiable and memorable
★ Suit you and your music
★ Be brilliantly executed

They could also:

★ Be a new twist on an old style
★ Be very simple and start a whole new dance craze

Some inside gen from a professional...

Paul Domaine
star choreographer

It may not have escaped your notice that I have been passed over for a guest appearance on 'Strictly Come Dancing'; there's a good reason for that and guess what, I've never had a dance lesson in my life! My advice on 'Killer Moves' comes from decades of experience and seeing what works generally when you're looking to promote an artist or record, but whenever I have needed to help an act with their 'Killer Moves' I have always called in a professional like Paul Domaine.

Paul has worked with everyone from Steps to Tina Turner and I asked him some questions about the process.

PW: **When you meet an artist you are going to work with for the first time, what are the top three qualities you hope that they have?**

PD: 1. Rhythm! I just hope that they have rhythm and they can keep in time. Just because someone can sing, doesn't always mean they can dance! As long as they can keep to the beat then I can make them move!

2. A Positive Attitude – it's very hard to teach someone a routine when they are negative when learning steps. It's so much easier to teach someone who wants to learn!

3. Potential – it's so rewarding when an artist begins to improve, picking up routines and improving on their overall performance. If they are not trained dancers or have never danced before it usually it takes a couple of singles for them to get comfortable with the routines and choreography.

PW: **Which artist or artists would you rate as having the best ever 'Killer Moves'?**

PD: Justin Timberlake and Usher. Justin has always been an amazing dancer even when he was in NSYNC. He makes everything look so easy and effortless. He has been so successful because he is an all-rounder, he has the 'Whole package'; he can dance, he sings, he writes and is a fantastic live performer. He has that 'Star Quality' that artists need to become so successful in the industry. Usher is also one of these artists, he has made some brilliant dance videos, again he knows how to sell a performance.

PW: **Of the current chart artists who do you rate?**

PD: Beyoncé and Justin Timberlake

PW: **Who has been your favourite artist to work with and why?**

PD: I've worked with many artists over the years … Sugababes, Five, Tina Turner, Westlife, Steps, George Michael, Lionel Ritchie, Michael Bolton, The Saturdays and Queen, but my favourite has to be Cher. After all the years in the industry she still has such a hunger for performing. She was a real 'Pro' who wanted to get everything right and was willing to listen to advice on every aspect. What also made her special was that she was such a lovely person, not only to me but to all the dancers who worked with her.

PW: **And if you could work with anyone in the history of pop music, who would it be and why?**

PD: Michael Jackson. I would love to have had the chance to work with him as he was such an amazing artist. A pop legend who inspired many people to perform.

Stage Presence and Camera Technique

You'll remember back at the start of this chapter I told you not to despair if you had two left feet. There are other ways to make an impression on stage and on screen and we're just about to look at them, but a few words of advice before we do. Don't write yourself off as a dancer without actually trying – you may be surprised at what a good teacher can get out of you. Get into shape with some form of sport or exercise – your body is an important part of your equipment.

However, with or without some classic 'Killer Moves' what you are going to need is stage presence and camera technique, and once again don't suppose that it just comes naturally. You can learn so much from watching the best and I can guarantee that all of the artists I'm about to mention will have thought through every move and having discovered what works for them will have made that move their trademark.

Westlife

As a case in point I'm starting with a band who rarely seem to do anything more ambitious than to get up and down from their stools – go back and look again. That simple move is just as choreographed as a more complicated routine and positioned for maximum impact within the song. They are also masters of camera technique – it's no accident that they sing straight down the camera to you (yes you personally!). Practice yourself at home – get a friend to video you moving around you (a mobile phone camera will do the job) and see how natural you can make your performance, but still make contact with the audience the other side of the lens.

Mick Jagger

The ancient rocker is still strutting and running around massive arena stages – but when he first took to the stage his pouting and almost uncoordinated moves made him the subject of many a mocking review. Fast forward several decades and just consider how many of today's rock acts owe something to his stage presence.

Elvis Presley

If your image of Elvis is of the bloated figure in rhinestone costumes playing out the end of his career in Vegas, or the cheesy Technicolor film star, think again and go back to what started the whole thing. Find some early footage of him curling his lip, brandishing his guitar and gyrating those hips as he performs 'Jailhouse Rock' or 'Heartbreak Hotel'. None of Elvis's moves could be described as dance – but they are possibly the most effective 'Killer Moves' of all time.

Stage presence is all about conviction and belief – but it is affected by the tiny details, the way you stand – or take the microphone from the stand – think about all of those things in your own performance and watch and learn from your favourite artists. If choreographed routines are never going to be your thing then make sure you have a 'Killer Walk', a 'Killer Stance' or even a 'Killer Lip Cur'l for the camera.

Check out Victoria Beckham's signature 'finger pointing' or Duffy's finger clicking, and when was the last time you saw Mariah Carey move much on stage – they all have great stage presence.

And here's a final tip, if you are the next Gary Barlow and have great songs and a great voice but are distinctly average in the dance studio then get yourself into a band that has some amazing dancers and with a bit of luck no-one will notice!

I'm going to audition for X Factor/Britain's Got Talent

Pete's Top Tips

You can have no idea just how many people I have seen auditioning on shows like Pop Idol where they think they know the routine because they have danced along with the star in question. When they stand in front of the judges they clearly and embarrassingly don't.

Clearing enough space in your bedroom or anywhere else in the house to dance in front of the DVD or computer is a great start, BUT once you think you know the routine turn your back on the TV and look into a mirror – as large a one as you can get – and practice, practice, practice until you think you really have the routine down perfectly. Then turn away from the mirror and get a friend to video you so you can watch it back. Watch it critically and see if you look as good as you feel – give yourself marks out of ten – unless it's at least a nine, it's not good enough.

Once you have a vocabulary of dance steps it's not such a stretch to put your own routine together, but here's another big reminder – you will have to sing at the same time as you dance and for that you don't want to be out of breath! Mastering this trick is a combination of fitness, practice and clever choreography. Many of today's artists will in fact mime a section of their live performances to backing track simply in order for them to include more challenging choreography. At a live audition you certainly won't have that option so practice your routine and sing at the same time.

It's also no good being perfect in your trainers and tracksuit if your 'Look' involves three-inch platforms and a miniskirt. You need to suit the choreography to your level of ability, music and style.

And finally rehearse in the outfit you will be auditioning in and that includes hair and make-up. There is nothing more guaranteed to poleaxe a promising audition than a wardrobe malfunction, a hair style that either collapses or flies into your eyes obscuring your vision or make-up that melts under the studio lights. And in case you find yourself crying tears of frustration, despair or hopefully, joy on camera always wear waterproof mascara!

More stuff that you can do…

Get inspired by this year's winners of Britain's Got Talent, Diversity, and get out there and find out what's going on in your community.

Get inspired by any number of films that focus on dance – just Google 'dance films' and do your own research, but here are just a few of the hundreds you can watch. Once again I make no apologies for including mostly golden oldies alongside more current offerings; remember what I said about reinventing a classic style?

'Chicago' – musical featuring Katherine Zeta Jones and Renee Zellwegger

'You Got Served' – LA Street Dance

'West Side Story' – period piece but a dance master class none the less

'Flashdance' – Jennifer Beals transforms from welder to Flashdancer

'High School Musical' – the clue is in the title
'Fame' – the original 'high school musical'

'Mad Hot Ballroom' – Ballroom dancing goes from lame to cool for a tough group of New York City school kids

'Dirty Dancing' – camp but classic

'Strictly Ballroom' – Young Australian hopefuls battle for victory at the Pan Europeans

'Grease' – classic 50's period piece

'Saturday Night Fever' – Adult content but classic 70's disco

Anything by Buzby Berkely or featuring Fred Astaire

Still can't dance? Then get yourself an iconic hand gesture and perfect your camera technique.

PUBLIC APPEAL

AND THE ALL IMPORTANT FAME FACTOR GRID SCORES...

Isn't this Fame Factor 10 – 'Public Appeal' just made up of a lot of the others you may ask yourself? Well, to an extent yes, but there is still more you can do to increase your chances of success and more importantly to sustain your career.

In this final chapter we discuss what that is, what you can do to ensure that you have maximum 'Public Appeal' and I reveal how my ten pop icons measure up to this and all 10 elements of the Fame Factor Grid. Remember that these are my opinions; you may think differently and can argue the case with your friends, but I also want you to think about how they apply to you.

In the case of the TV talent shows, winning public support is everything and surely people are just voting for the most talented contestants? Well, to some degree they are, but there's another slightly more intangible force at work here; one that the TV producers exploit to maximum effect in the way the show is shot and edited.

Paul Potts was the first winner of Britain's Got Talent in June 2007, by Christmas of the same year Gordon Brown was presenting him with a platinum disc for 2 million sales of his debut album. He had been passionate about singing all his life, singing opera with amateur companies and had even paid to go to Italy and take a master class with Pavarotti. But the audience knew none of this as he presented himself on stage for the audition in Cardiff.

In the VT excerpt that accompanied his performance the TV producers portrayed him as a quiet little man rather lacking in self-confidence as he stepped awkwardly onto the stage to audition in Cardiff. In other words our expectations were lowered and in fact we were a bit anxious that this nice man wasn't about to make a fool of himself; which made the total shock of when he opened his mouth and let fly his moving rendition of 'Nessun Dorma' even more effective.

Many of the audience, including judge, Amanda Holden, were reduced to tears and it wasn't all about the power of his singing, it was a combination of relief, surprise and delight. Paul Potts was someone the audience could identify with, an ordinary chap with a typical job, but someone who had the chance to escape with an unexpected talent. He became the next day's 'water cooler' moment, everyone was talking about him and the papers loved him. From that point on, and even before we discovered in the semi finals that singing had been his only solace when he was bullied at school, the public willed him to win and voted in droves.

But let's not run away with the idea that the only route to success is via a TV talent show. As you've seen already there are many roads to success

Stuff that you can do...

Let's assume that you have: 'The Songs', a 'Distinctive Voice', 'The Look', 'Killer Moves' and 'PR'ability'; what else can you do to appeal to the public? Here are a few golden rules:

★ Be yourself – the fans will soon see through a fake persona.

★ Be nice to your fans – make time for them, you truly are nothing without them.

★ Be nice to the people you work with and the professionals you meet – this is a surprisingly small business and it's amazing how a bad reputation spreads, especially in these days of instant web access.

★ Be professional – if a TV producer is only 90% convinced by your new record, the fact that he liked you when you appeared on the show last time and knows he can rely on you for a sparkling performance may convince him to book you; and may be the difference as to whether your record is a hit or not.

★ Don't change your style too quickly or too drastically – don't underestimate the time it takes for the general public to latch on to who you are; if you change too quickly you'll only confuse them.

★ Be prepared or chill out – if you are out in public you are going to get photographed and you can't control whose Facebook those shots are going to appear on, no matter how hard you try. So just get over it and make sure you always look good or go out in disguise!

★ Listen to the professionals – you may not always be able to see what it is about you that is so appealing to the public.

★ Remember, every interview is as important as the next and may be the first time the public are hearing or reading about you.

★ Always play the hits – you may be a bit bored with them, but your fans are not – and that's what they paid to come and hear.

★ And finally, turn the page to see how I scored my 10 pop icons on the Fame Factor Grid and which particular Fame Factors make them so appealing to the public.

There's a blank row for you to fill in again. Having read the book is your score the same as when we started this journey? What can you do to get a perfect 10?

FINAL SCORES ON THE FAME FACTOR GRID

★ I've a completed the grid awarding each pop icon a star for the Fame Factors they possess.

★ Sometimes I've only awarded half a star for a particular Fame Factor.

	1. The Songs	2. A Distinctive Voice	3. The Look	4. Determination	5. Stamina
Michael Jackson	★	☆	☆	☆	☆
Madonna	☆	★	☆	☆	☆
Lady Gaga	☆	⯪	★	☆	
Simon Cowell			☆	★	☆
Kylie Minogue	☆	☆	☆	☆	★
Spice Girls	☆	⯪	☆	☆	☆
Robbie Williams	☆	☆	☆	☆	☆
Girls Aloud	☆	⯪	☆	☆	☆
Beyonce Knowles	☆	☆	☆	☆	☆
Leona Lewis	⯪	☆	☆	☆	
YOU					

★ I've added up my pop icons' Fame Factor scores in the right hand column.

★ Finally, now that you know a lot more about what it takes to become a pop star – how does your score measure up?

6. PR'ability	7. Self Belief	8. Supporting Cast	9. Killer Moves	10. Public Appeal	Fame Factor Score
☆	☆	☆	☆	☆	10
☆	☆	☆	☆	☆	10
☆	☆	☆	☆		7½
☆	☆			☆	6
☆	☆	☆	☆	☆	10
★	☆	☆	☆	☆	9½
☆	⭑	☆	☆	☆	9½
☆	☆	★	☆	☆	9½
☆	☆	☆	★	☆	10
	☆	☆		★	6½

MY 10 POP ICONS...

Their Public Appeal and Fame Factor scores!

Michael Jackson

Despite Michael Jackson's increasingly bizarre behaviour in his later years and some very negative headlines, he still managed to sell out 50 nights at London's 02 Arena immediately they went on sale. Proof, in case it were needed, of his enduring 'Public Appeal' that will only be heightened by his sad early demise.

For me his extra appeal lies in the originality and the creativity he applied to all his performances'. He was my icon who best embodied Fame Factor 1 – 'The Songs' but in the first draft of this chapter I gave him a Fame Factor overall score of 9½ as I had a question mark over his stamina as he approached that run of 50 shows booked for the summer of 2009. Sadly, my misgivings were proved correct, but now I am reverting to the Michael Jackson who dazzled on previous tours and am scoring him a perfect 10!

Madonna

I chose Madonna to illustrate Fame Factor 2 – 'A Distinctive Voice'. The fact that so much has been said about Madonna's ability to change her look, persona and keep re-inventing herself makes it no less true or effective as a way of constantly keeping the public's interest. She also became a gay icon with 'Vogue' early in her career.

I really couldn't mark her down on any of the Fame Factors so Madonna also scores a perfect 10.

Lady Gaga

As a relatively new artist it's hard to gauge what Lady Gaga's enduring 'Public Appeal' will be, but having Fame Factor 3 – 'The Look' has certainly got her the initial attention that enables the public to start a relationship with her.

It's clear that she has some great songs and the 'Determination' to break out of being a backroom writer to becoming the centre stage star, but I just don't know at this stage whether she has the long term 'Stamina' or 'Public Appeal' or quite how much of a 'Distinctive Voice' she will turn out to have (hence a half mark for this Fame Factor). I am guessing that she has a good 'Supporting Cast' to have got as far as she has and altogether I've given her a Fame Factor score of 7½, but I will be quite happy if she proves me wrong and turns out to have a perfect score.

Simon Cowell

I picked Simon as my example of Fame Factor 4 – 'Determination' but his 'Public Appeal' is his honesty. Because praise from him is hard won it is valued so much more when it is given. He may not be right 100% of the time, but people trust him and want to hear what the has to say; and when he turns on the charm he is very charismatic.

OK, so he only has a Fame Factor of 6, but his fame doesn't depend on him being able to perform in the usual sense of the word. He's a good looking guy, and clearly doesn't need the 'Voice', 'Songs' or 'Killer Moves' for his fame as a TV personality (although his long term success depends on being able to pick the hits). And if anyone doubts his 'Stamina' they should never challenge him to a 'press-ups' competition! His physical fitness is indicative of his drive and determination. I haven't give him a Fame Factor star for 'Supporting Cast' because although he has great people working for him, Simon is in many ways a one man band, preferring to making his crucial decisions himself.

Kylie

At the beginning of her pop career people could identify with Kylie as the girl next door and even in 1988 she won a Logie for the most popular person on Australian TV and we found ourselves having to write the duet 'Especially For You' for her and Jason due to enormous public demand. A duet that neither Kylie or Jason were that keen on, our conviction that it was what the public wanted was proven when the record shot straight to number 1!

However glamourous Kylie has become, whenever she is interviewed on TV, she proves that she is still a lovely, accessible person with whom people clearly still identify. Her early hi-energy records gained a devoted following in the gay clubs and the theatricality of her shows ensures her continued position as a pink pin up. I chose Kylie as my example of Fame Factor 5 – 'Stamina' and surprise, surprise Kylie scores a perfect 10 – is anyone going to argue with me?

Spice Girls

We talked about the Spice Girls appeal a lot in Fame Factor 6 – 'PR'ability' but just to recap; five girls with five very different personas were cast to appeal to as many different types of fans as possible. On top of which they hit on their battle cry of 'Girl Power' and totally captured the public's imagination, encouraging thousands of little girls to think that they too could follow their dreams and one day be a Spice Girl or whatever else they wanted to be.

However, they miss out on a perfect score by half a mark on the basis that even though you could just about tell who was who on the records, I don't think any of the girls had a truly 'Distinctive Voice' (with the possible exception of Mel C) so I deducted half a mark for that Fame Factor, giving them a total of 9½.

Robbie Williams

Robbie's ability to flip from superstar entertainer on stage to exposing his weaknesses and insecurities offstage, without ever taking himself too seriously, is a winning combination. It allows his fans to adore him yet still feel some empathy with him. He's a flawed hero which is why we love him.

I chose him as my icon to illustrate Fame Factor 7 – 'Self-belief' but in the end I can only really award him half a star for this Fame Factor – so he also falls just sort of full marks with another 9½.

Girls Aloud

Girls Aloud were my illustration of Fame Factor 8 – 'Supporting Cast' but they also manage to pull off the trick of being incredibly impressive and glamourous in their videos and stage shows whilst still retaining an element of approachability. This was, of course, helped by their original path to stardom as people feel they know them and have personally contributed to their success. The girls still give the impression that with a bit of application and good luck we could be them and living their glamorous life.

However, I docked the girls half a point on 'Distinctive Voice' as I think that only Nadine has a truly 'Distinctive Voice'. Girls Aloud score 9½.

Beyoncé

Beyoncé proves that you don't always have to be accessible to have 'Public Appeal' as her appeal is her absolute star quality. There are very few of us who think we could be her. She is a diva; she delivers on all the Fame Factor elements, especially Fame Factor 9 – 'Killer Moves', and gets full marks on the Fame Factor grid.

Leona Lewis

Leona looks gorgeous and has a brilliant voice which is why so many people voted for her to win X Factor. Therefore it seems a contradiction to say that she doesn't necessarily have huge 'Public Appeal', even though I picked her to illustrate that particular Fame Factor! However, I personally feel that I still don't know anything more about Leona than I did at the end of the show, or have a real connection with her. It will be interesting to see whether her 'Look' and 'Distinctive Voice' will be enough to sustain a long and successful career.

She gets a lowish 6½ because I have only starred her on the Fame Factors I feel she has displayed to date and she has only had two great songs so far with 'A Moment Like This' and 'Bleeding Love'. I look forward to seeing how her career and her Fame Factors progress.

And Finally...

★ Pick your top 5 favourite stars and really think about why you like them over all the artists you could have chosen.

★ What is it about them that made you notice them in the first place?

★ What made you really like them?

★Is there anything you can learn from them and apply to yourself?

Everyone needs that lucky break…

Well do you? It's another well worn cliché but to me it's much more about making your own luck and having a positive attitude.

I promise you there will not be a single successful artist who didn't have several major disappointments on their road to success. The question is how you deal with them and move on.

In the same way there are many failed artists who simply didn't recognise an opportunity when it presented itself.

So…

Think about the advice in this book and always look for the positive, if you do you'll put yourself in the best possible position to leap on that 'lucky break' when it comes along.

Go for it!

All the best

Pete

WEBSITES FOR ADDITIONAL INFORMATION

in alphabetical order, and what they say about themselves…

AIM - The Association of Independent Music
www.musicindie.com

The Association of Independent Music is a non-profit-making trade organisation for independent record companies and distributors in the UK. Their job is to help our individual members' businesses, and to support the needs of the independent sector. They do this through information, advice seminars mentoring, networking, legal and business affairs guidance, work experience schemes, commercial negotiation, lobbying and bargaining, opening access to international markets.

A&R Worldwide
www.anrworldwide.com

A&R Worldwide encompasses an unprecedented network of globe-spanning relationships and insider music industry knowledge, delivering a one-stop solution for talent discovery, development, consulting and marketing services—helping clients make inroads on multiple levels throughout an ever-evolving musical ecosystem.

BPI and Brit School
www.bpi.co.uk

The BPI is the representative voice of the UK recorded music business. It organises the annual BRIT Awards show as well as the Classical BRIT Awards show.

The BRIT School is Britain's only FREE Performing Arts and Technology School. It is an independent, state funded City College for the Technology of the Arts, the only one of its kind dedicated to education and vocational training for the performing arts, media, art and design and the technologies that make performance possible. They are not a stage or fame school but a vocational school; if an applicant is determined on a life devoted to art, dance, music, radio, television/film or theatre, then this could well be the right place.

BBC – One Music
www.bbc.co.uk/radio1/onemusic

Information on how to make it in music.

Billboard Magazine
www.billboard.com

Online publication for the USA music business.

International Managers Forum
www.musicmanagersforum.co.uk

The IMF has given managers an opportunity for sharing and learning and also a much-needed voice within the industry. The forum has provided a chance for meaningful dialogue with the Government and other industry organisations as well as between managers themselves.

Meta
www.metamusic.org.uk

The Meta project brings together music makers and workers across the British Isles and is a good information resource.

Music Tank

www.musictank.co.uk

MusicTank, a business development network for the UK music industry, owned and operated by the University of Westminster - its purpose; to engage with industry, innovation and change across the music business.

Music Week

www.musicweek.com

Weekly online publication for the UK music business.

Musicians Union

www.musiciansunion.org.uk

The Musicians' Union represents over thirty thousand musicians working in all sectors of the music business. As well as negotiating on behalf of their members with all the major employers in the industry, they offer a range of services for professional and student musicians of all ages.

Perez Hilton

www.perezhilton.com

An up to the minute insight into the world of celebrity. All things music, TV, Film and fashion come under the harshest scrutiny or the highest praise. On here you will learn how to get into the good books of one of the worlds ruthless celebrity critics, and pick up a number of tips of what not to do along the way to stardom.

Popjustice
www.popjustice.com

For everything you ever needed to know about pop music, past, present and future. Founded by one of the UK's most respected music journalists, Peter Robinson (NME, The Guardian), this website offers an honest breakdown of what does and what doesn't make great pop music.

Record of The Day
www.recordoftheday.com

Record of the Day is the music industry's favourite daily digest providing a raft of original and aggregated news from all UK and international media outlets, encompassing press and online. Each daily mailout also contains a sound clip of the best in new music chosen by the RotD team. The company also produces a weekly music industry magazine containing comment, news, data, listings, interviews and of course, clips to the best new music out there.

This Day In Music
www.thisdayinmusic.com

This Day in Music lists just about every significant event that happened in music on everyday of the year from the 50's to the present day.

If you've enjoyed this book, visit

www.thefamefactor.co.uk

for additional features, content
and comment